Fitness and Sports Competition for the Older Adult

Charles E. "Chuck" DePaepe

VANTAGE PRESS
New York

The opinions expressed herein are solely those of the author.

FIRST EDITION

All rights reserved, including the right of
reproduction in whole or in part in any form.

Copyright © 2003 by Charles E. "Chuck" DePaepe

Published by Vantage Press, Inc.
516 West 34th Street, New York, New York 10001

Manufactured in the United States of America
ISBN: 0-533-14481-7

Library of Congress Catalog Card No.: 2002095622

0 9 8 7 6 5 4 3 2 1

Contents

Introduction   v

One	Introduction to Good Health	1
Two	Trimming Down	10
Three	Choices	26
Four	Running	30
Five	Swimming	42
Six	Cycling	71
Seven	Triathlons	96
Eight	Injuries	119

Appendix: Composition of Foods   135

Introduction

The human body is a wonderful creation of interrelated systems and functions. It is complex and not fully understood. We cannot completely describe it, and what knowledge exists has been developed to a substantial extent by those admirable doctors, researchers, and the authors of the literature covering the subject. Nevertheless, we can at least describe how to care for it, in simple terms related to aerobics and ultimate fitness. It is appropriate that we should try to understand, as best we can, how to care for this exquisite form—the product of two humans, nurtured into life to subsequently fend for itself. We are all part of that life cycle.

Exercise in which all of us partake, even the most sedentary, requires energy. For energy, we consume food in the form of solids and liquids, including water and oxygen. The amount and quality of the food, water, and oxygen we take in must be sufficient to adequately support the system.

The body can store food and water, but can store only a limited amount of oxygen (muscles in good condition can store greater amounts). The body will continue to be productive for only a few minutes if its oxygen is cut off. Consequently, we have to constantly breathe to acquire the oxygen needed. When we first begin to exercise, we use up the little bit of oxygen that is stored, and as that supply is quickly depleted (anaerobically), we must depend on the oxygen to be replenished by breathing.

Our lungs add oxygen to our blood, which is pumped by our heart through the blood vessels to the various parts of the body, including the muscles. Therefore, the lungs, heart, cardiovascular system, and the muscles have so very much to do with our overall health, and, of course, our aerobic capability. Those who are *not* fit cannot utilize the oxygen intake required to function well. On the other hand, those who are fit have bodies that can develop oxygen in amounts that will support high levels of achievement.

The process of developing endurance and fitness requires a proper diet and the ability to increase the supply of oxygen to our body. The oxygen increase happens when we improve muscle tone and fitness, which requires training ourselves. Training demands pushing ourselves through considerable effort and some discomfort. Aerobic levels will increase as the little storehouses of energy within our blood cells increase. (Anaerobic and aerobic levels will be described later.) The process entails changing our lifestyle, which brings with it the rewards and joy of being in the upper level of physical well-being in our society. This book describes, very simply, how to become fit (and be a better person) both in a physical and mental sense.

One
Introduction to Good Health

We were standing around before a bicycle race one day, just talking. An elderly lady was overheard talking about her eighty-three-year-old husband as he was about to enter a race. She said, "I keep talking to him. He is too old to be out there racing, but the old fool won't listen." And we wondered who the fool was. Statement made by unknown bikers.

A New Outlook

For most of us who are older, competitive sports is a form of recreation. Winning is important, but it is not everything. Nevertheless, each of us tries to do our best, and placing in a race always gives a sense of elation. That elation is not because we have beaten someone to the finish line, but because we have in some way increased our ability to improve. And, let's face it, we—all of us—like to look good. Personal records, when achieved, especially as we grow older, are without a doubt important. Who knows, we may continue to improve or at least excel when we are well into our eighties! In a 1996 local Senior Olympics, a ninety-year-old lady ran the 50-meter dash in something like eleven seconds!

Do you want to look and feel better? Are you tired and bored with watching TV? Did you know that if you were slim and trim you might outdo what you see on those soaps? Suppose you stand out in the crowd, and the kids and grandkids notice it. Wouldn't that make you want to do handsprings? Then, you could invite them to the next race. Can you imagine running a 5K (3.1 miles) with the adults and then running a 1-miler with your six- or seven-year-old grandchild? When some young aspiring athlete comes up to you and says, "I noticed you ran the 5K and then ran the 1-miler with little Rachel. How do you do it?" You reply, "Shucks, it was no big deal." Well, folks, we're not selling snake oil here. We're not here to sell books either. There is no magic elixir to put you in shape to enjoy a higher quality of life. But, getting fit is a goal that is attainable for all who, within their capabilities, are willing to work at it on a regular basis.

Common Sense

No one should enter any sports program without approval from a doctor (a cardiologist, a sports doctor, or one who stays fit through exercise would be an excellent choice). If your doctor says you can enter into a fitness program, and you do so as part of your lifestyle, you have entered into your first major fitness accomplishment. Your doctor will jump up and down for joy, for he or she will have helped you with your first step, which usually makes them feel good when they go home at the end of a long day.

Getting started is tough. Later, we will discuss why many who get started in a fitness program do not continue. Whether you choose to be a runner, biker, a swimmer, or participate in any other fitness activity, you may find that after a few weeks of training or conditioning, continuing on remains difficult. Here is where most good intentions go by the wayside. Making physical exercise work for you will require a change in your lifestyle. Staying with a well thought-out program for just six weeks will bring marvelous results. You will feel better, your step will be livelier. All of a sudden you're a better person, and that includes how you feel mentally. Now you are hooked, and what's really great is that there are a lot of physical and mental rewards ahead—that is, if you stick with the program.

No athletic or fitness program can be complete without giving some consideration to diet. Some "natural" athletes get by with eating junk foods and even eating too soon before a strenuous event. Some can party all night and win a race the next day. If you think you are one of these, stop reading here, for what follows is for the rest of us—those of us who must conform with the rules of common sense, which may not be so common after all.

Most of us already into a senior's sport or exercise program got into it without much advice or without knowing or observing basic rules and procedures. We just went out and did it. Needless to say, most of us had a variety of painful injuries. The pain is always twofold: the actual muscle pain, and the mental frustration of having to take time off to heal. Cases can be cited about those who kept going out again before the healing process was completed and how they re-injured themselves until there was permanent damage. So, they were out of the picture for good. Obviously, common sense should prevail with all of the personal discipline we can muster.

There are about as many training programs and theories as there are coaches—maybe more. A lot of literature covers the subject. This book does not provide many methods of training; rather, it provides some theory, guidelines, and rules that will help those preparing to go into quality fitness programs or endurance sports. How closely you follow what is presented here depends on how serious you are and how interested you are about progressing into an injury-free exercise program. And, even if you're careful, you may have an injury once in a while as you try to stretch your capabilities. Some practical rules and guidelines along with nutritional information will help you over the hurdles.

Years ago, through the efforts of Dr. Kenneth Cooper, it was determined that a good exercise program would greatly enhance an individual's health. The motivating concern was that so many members of the population were becoming sedentary.[1] Much as been written since, and more knowledge continues to be added. Dr. Cooper's basic findings still hold true, and if you want to extend your limits, there are higher levels, which are enticing to those of us who want to excel. You do not need to be competitive

1. Kenneth H. Cooper, M.D., *Aerobics,* New York, Bantam Books, 1968.

to enjoy the benefits. Many men and women enter a race for the pure joy of expressing their physical fitness and enjoying the camaraderie that is associated with others who feel the same way.

How the Body Develops Energy

Understanding the body's muscular output is a bit complex. It's a three-part process that can best be understood if we analyze each part. It will be to your advantage to take the time to understand the process involved in getting those muscles to put out the energy you need in your sport of choice. Understanding the process (not necessarily all of the technical intricacies) will give you a leg up on how to run, bike, or swim your next event. The three-part muscular energy output applies to young and old alike; just remember, everything happens a little slower with older folks because your joints and muscles are less flexible, and your lungs are operating at a somewhat reduced capacity. Gender makes no difference except, as a rule, men are usually stronger than women. Think about that the next time a fragile-looking gal passes you in a race!

That First Energy Burst. This is the technical stuff, which is based on medical literature. If you want to get serious and excel, especially in competition, it will be necessary to understand the basics of the body's process of providing energy output. Your body contains a high-energy molecule called adenosine triphosphate (ATP). It consists of a base, adenine; a sugar, ribose; and three phosphate groups. Breaking the bond between two phosphate units releases energy to the muscles. We have a limited storage capacity for ATP, and during a maximum rate of activity, this energy is depleted in a few seconds.

The body has three interrelated metabolic processes for continually resupplying this molecule. The process used depends on the muscle's energy needs at a given moment and on the duration of the activity. The most immediately available source for reconstructing ATP is phosphocreatine, a high-energy bearing molecule. The energy release by the breakdown of the phosphocreatine molecule is used to resynthesize ATP. The phosphocreatine system can recharge ATP for only a short while—just for about five to ten seconds during a sprint. When this supply is exhausted, the body must rely on two other ATP generating processes—one that does not require oxygen, "anaerobic," and one that does, "aerobic." At the start of a vigorous physical effort, you use up this first important energy burst.

The Anaerobic Energy Burst. This second energy source is known as *glycolysis*. During this period of energy output, you will not yet be breathing hard. Cells will break down carbohydrates (glucose or glycogen in the muscle) to release energy for replenishing the ATP molecule.

The anaerobic metabolism of carbohydrates builds up lactic acid in the muscles within about two minutes, which causes burning muscle discomfort. It is at this point that many decide that the discomfort is peculiar only to them and that they should not continue. An endurance athlete will always know when this discomfort happens. The lactic acid and its metabolite, lactate, accumulates in the muscle, but this condition does not always reduce performance. Through training, elite competitors (and some of us not so elite), learn to tolerate the discomfort and continue on (see note). However, the lactic acid and lactate eventually begin to stop the muscles from functioning. This anaerobic process only takes place for a short time and cannot be depended upon for endurance events.

> ***Note:*** *A distinction between discomfort and pain should be made here. Discomfort is sensed when the muscle fibers are stretched without tearing. Think of pain as evidence of an injury that occurs when the muscle fibers tear.*

After a few minutes, your body will have to depend upon a third source of energy, which is called aerobic energy.

The transition from the anaerobic level to the next level, the aerobic level, we will call the lower anaerobic threshold.

The Aerobic Process. This process takes care of your energy supply over the long haul. Some athletes, properly trained, can continue to compete at high intensity levels for many hours. The aerobic process involves the breakdown of carbohydrates, fat, and protein. This system does not switch on quickly and does not do so until one or two minutes of hard exercise has occurred. An increase in breathing and heart rates then occurs, ensuring delivery of oxygen to the muscle cells. After this aerobic process kicks in, the athlete must select a pace to stabilize the breathing and heart rate, at which time the athlete is truly aerobic. In the meantime, the other two systems function at a lower level, storing energy in less active muscles. You can then use this stored energy for that final burst needed at the end of a race or for that additional effort necessary to make the top of the next hill.

The aerobic process is very efficient, but its ability to supply muscles with energy has an upper limit. This limit is called the aerobic threshold. It's the point where your body goes into the anaerobic level again. The limit can be best described as when your breathing rate increases and does not level off, because you're pushing yourself harder or because going up a hill requires more energy. That's when the other two energy sources must kick in. You may reach this upper limit several times during an endurance event. Just remember, these first two sources of ATP only provide for short-term bursts of energy, and if you push too hard you may have to stop or slow way down. After each "sprint," your body should then return to the aerobic process. Understanding these three sources of energy and how they work will help you master your capabilities during a race or a strenuous fitness session.

Training Concepts

Training involves improving endurance, speed, and strength. These qualities will require the fitness enthusiast to make improvements in the sport of his or her choice. Each of these aspects of a sport should be considered for the specific event in which each individual chooses to participate. For example, the long distance runner, swimmer, or biker will develop the three qualities for events such as the marathon, 1000-yard freestyle, and a 25-mile bike race. The sprinter must concentrate on improving short term endurance, speed, and strength. Short term endurance, speed, and strength are not the same as the qualities required in long-distance events.

That being said, one might ask, "What if I want to do both long and short distance events?" The answer is that you must train for both. But don't expect to excel in all of them. Almost all runners, swimmers, and bikers try to participate in races of various lengths. With a lot of training, some do quite well. The one hazard to training for most of the various distances is overtraining. National champions usually train for a few select events. The rest of us try to do most of them because of the enjoyment of being in all the local meets.

New training methods go back to the story of ancient Greece.[2] Milon of Croton would pick up a tiny calf and raise it over his head each day until the animal was fully grown. As he continued to extend himself, his strength grew, and he became the strongest man in the world.

The fundamental principle of training is that sustained activity to higher levels will adapt the muscles and the rest of your body to increased capabilities. You've heard the maxim, "No pain, no gain"? What that means is that you must extend yourself to get increased performance. To do so will involve some degree of discomfort (not pain), some of which was described as part of the lactic acid build-up during the anaerobic process. Training at higher levels does not mean that you should exercise at your aerobic limit. Training at 85 percent of your aerobic limit (maximum breathing rate), or as will be described later, at 85 percent of your maximum heart rate, will advance you to higher limits of performance. That means that long, slow runs and the discomfort you experience will give you the ability to go from point A to point B improving endurance—but you won't win any races.

The essence of improvement comes when you try or train to go from one point to the other more quickly. But, we must always remember that too much pain will result in injury. The trick is to

---

2. Jay T. Kearney, "Training the Olympic Athlete," *Scientific American*, New York, July 1966.

know when you're exceeding your own stress limits. And the limits are different for each of us. For those who are more competitive, and some of us who are not, our egos will get in the way, and we will exceed the limit and end up hurt; some of us will continue to do it, time after time.

Understanding the concepts of how your body uses the three forms of energy will help you develop in the sports of your choice. For example, a distance runner, biker, or swimmer should focus on aerobic capability. This athlete will pass through the first two bursts of energy and rely almost totally on the aerobic system. In contrast, a weight lifter will rely on short bursts of energy supplied by breaking the bond of the phosphate groups, that first energy boost. Racket ball, badminton, tennis, and other sports will use combinations of the three energy sources.

As previously stated, increasing the level of effort for an endurance sport requires increasing the levels of stress, and often enduring discomfort, thereby improving performance. While training methods vary, numerous factors play a role in achieving athletic excellence. These factors must always prevail regardless of the training method. Here are a few of the important rules to guide you:

1. Maintain a proper diet.
2. Get adequate rest.
3. Avoid overtraining (see note).
4. Take the time to reach your goals.
5. Use proper equipment.
6. Warm up and cool down.
7. Find a mentor, if you can.
8. Conduct a sensible program.

***Note:** Overtraining occurs when your body does not get enough rest in between training sessions. Overtraining results in poorer times, reduced endurance, and lower levels of strength. Overtraining is often caused by training above 85 percent of your maximum heart rate.*

The Aging Process

No sports book would be complete without a discussion on aging. Aging is a nonreversible process that affects all of us. Most of us don't like it, but it's going on whether we like it or not. Exercise will not stop our physical decline due to aging, but it will slow its rate. Being fit will give all of us a better quality of life. It's sad that many of those who lead sedentary lifestyles either don't know that life can be better and more fulfilling, or they don't have the desire to do anything about it.

Those who study aging (gerontologists) have had a rule of thumb that after the age of twenty-five there is a decline in our physical attributes of about one percent per year. This decline includes oxygen intake, strength, and endurance. Studies of the general population verified this conclusion. However, studies conducted with Masters Swimmers (competitive swimmers throughout the U.S. in all age groups in five-year groupings) revealed that the one percent rule applied to a population that was basically sedentary.

Dr. Phillip Whiten has conducted studies of Masters Swimmers using performances from 1975.[3] His studies indicate that the physical capabilities of aging Masters Swimmers is well below the one percent decline. That is good news for those of us over fifty. These studies provide evidence that a program of exercise is beneficial as long as we participate in an aerobic sport.

---

3. Dr. Phillip Whiten, *The Complete Book of Swimming,* New York, Random House, 1994.

Two
Trimming Down

Reaching goals includes understanding what has to be done and how to do it, and you must have the desire to get there. You must be convinced; then, you must be stubborn.

Obesity and Diet

Obesity is a problem for a large segment of our society. Approximately thirty-five percent of our society is overweight to some degree. Obesity is especially serious for anyone contemplating entering into a strenuous endurance activity. It is well documented that mortality rates increase with weight. Obesity is a more serous risk factor than that of smoking or high blood pressure, according to Dr. William Castelli, Director of the Framingham (Massachusetts) Heart Study.

Dieting to eliminate obesity is a complex process. Medical experts do not know all the answers. Losing excess weight can, however, be reduced to some fundamentals. We need food to function. To function properly, we need the right *kinds* of food in the right *amounts*. Therefore, two things need to happen; we need to restrict our food intake (reducing calories), and we need to eat the right kinds of food (nutrition is an important factor). All of which is easier said than done.

Generally, overweight people will be limited to how well they can do in sports. Those who are overweight are often embarrassed by their appearance. Accordingly, thousands attempt weight loss through the many diet programs that exist. Diets for the most part end up in failure; ninety percent or more of those who diet regain all or most of their lost weight in five years or less.

To further complicate matters, genetics play an important part. If your parents were fat, then there is about an eighty percent chance that you will be pudgy. Conversely, skinny parents probably will beget skinny offspring. Of course, your genetic predisposition to be fat or skinny will also be influenced by the environment in which you live. Not many of us will move to Kenya where those skinny runners come from.

To make matters worse, *metabolism,* (the process of converting food into energy), will have a bearing on the athlete, wanna-be athlete, or fitness enthusiast. Recent information reveals that the body has a natural weight to which it wants to gravitate. The body tends to maintain that weight whenever it goes over or under that natural setpoint.

It is interesting and satisfying to know that your metabolic rate will increase with muscle conditioning and development. Metabolism will remain at an increased level for as long as eight hours after exercise.

Two notions, commonly held, need to be ignored: Dieting changes the metabolic process, making it difficult to lose weight, and fat people burn calories more slowly. Metabolism is controlled by that natural setpoint. But there is hope. Your natural setpoint can be reset, although how that occurs is not yet completely understood.

So far all this discussion about diet has been negative. Ultimately, most diets fail (for all of the reasons previously cited), and because hunger is a strong motivating force to which all of us eventually succumb. First of all, to overcome all of the obstacles, we need to understand that a restricted calorie intake and exercise, as a *combination,* are essential if you need to lose weight. Then, you will need to determine what it is you will put into your mouth.

Although you may be in good health, you should not reduce your daily calorie intake to less than 1500 calories, unless you do so with the approval of a physician. Nathan Pritikin promoted a rather strict ratio of carbohydrates, fat, and protein.[4] He suggested that 80 percent of food eaten should be made up of carbohydrates, but a calorie intake of 65 percent carbohydrates, 20

---

4. Nathan Pritikin, *The Pritikin Promise,* New York, Pocket Books, 1985.

percent fat, and 15 percent protein will give you pretty close the amount of minerals, vitamins, and the other stuff necessary to sustain adequate nutrition levels.

It is imperative that fat intake be restricted. Americans eat double the amount of fat recommended by nutritionists. Your ingestion of fat could be restricted by becoming a vegetarian, but most folks won't go that route. Well over 90 percent of the fat you eat ends up as fat in your body. To restrict fat intake, it will be necessary to learn to read labels on the containers of foods you buy. Primarily, the best way to reduce fat intake is to reduce the amount of red meat, butter, and the amount of coconut and palm oils you eat. We will have more to say on that later. Say good-bye to those greasy hamburgers and French fries.

Almost all the food you buy will come in packages that will identify the contents. The Food and Drug Administration has designed the nutrition label based on standard serving sizes and food intakes of 2000 and 2500 calories a day. This label is one of the best things that government has done since the Depression went out of style. It identifies calories and calories from fat for each serving. Also listed are total fat, saturated fat, cholesterol, sodium, total carbohydrates, dietary fiber, sugars, and protein in terms of grams or milligrams. Percentage of the daily values are listed and are based on a 2000-calorie-per-day intake. See Figure 1 for an example of a nutrition label.

You may wonder what calorie intake is right for you. Well, although there is no exact way to figure a precise value, there are tables from which you can determine what your calorie intake *should* be. For example, a male over fifty weighing about 150 pounds exerting moderate activity can be expected to burn about 2500 calories each day. A female under the same conditions can burn up to 2000 calories. Of course, athletes will burn more. Daily recommended values on the food container labels are based on 60 percent of the calories from carbohydrates, a total fat intake of 30 percent, and a protein intake of 10 percent.[5] In

---

5. "Nutrition, a Key to Good Health," *Information Plus,* Wylie, Texas, 1985 Edition.

Nutrition Facts

Serving Size: ½ cup (56 g) dry
Servings Per Container: 8

Amount Per Serving

Calories 210 Calories from Fat 10

	% Daily Value*
Total Fat 1 g	2%
Saturated Fat 0 g	0%
Polyunsaturated Fat 0.5 g	
Monounsaturated Fat 0 g	
Cholesterol 0 mg	0%
Sodium 0 mg**	0%
Total Carbohydrate 42 g	14%
Dietary Fiber 2 g	7%
Sugars 3 g	
Protein 7 g	

Vitamin A 0%	•	Vitamin C 0%
Calcium 0%	•	Iron 10%
Thiamin 30%	•	Riboflavin 10%
Niacin 15%		

*Percent Daily Values are based on a 2,000 calorie diet. Your daily values may be higher or lower depending on your calorie needs:

	Calories:	2,000	2,500
Total Fat	Less than	65g	80g
Saturated Fat	Less than	20g	25g
Cholesterol	Less than	300mg	300mg
Sodium	Less than	2,400mg	2,400mg
Total Carbohydrate		300g	375g
Dietary Fiber		25g	30g

Calories per gram:
Fat 9 • Carbohydrate 4 • Protein 4

INGREDIENTS: Semolina, Ferrous Sulfate, Niacinamide, Thiamin Mononitrate, Riboflavin
**Without added salt in cooking water.

Figure 1. Food and Drug Administration Label

this book, we recommend a 65-20-15 percent ratio, which is close to that given on food container labels. Pritikin had the right idea by promoting a stricter value for carbohydrates, but maybe he was a bit too strict.

Sound a bit too complicated? Reading and understanding the food labels takes a bit of effort, but it is very helpful in knowing what and how much to put into your mouth each day. If you look at the bottom of the label, you will find a conversion factor to convert grams into calories. As an example, if the label shows that a serving contains "13g" of fat, you can multiply the factor for fat, 9, times 13 to get 117 calories. You can do these conversions for each item on the label; but, if you are just interested in total calories per serving, you will find the value at the top of the label.

You do not need to be a dietitian or nutrition expert to understand your intakes. The label does most of the work for you. What you must do is to decide what and how much. It's a little easier when you know that fat is a major culprit. Reducing fat intake and substituting carbohydrates and protein will reduce your calorie intake because one gram of fat equals nine calories, and one gram of carbohydrates and protein each equal only four calories. It's a great trade-off; however, the body does need some fat for its nutritional balance. Nevertheless, most of us will go to the grave lusting for that greasy hamburger, and those of us who fall victim to that desire too often may get there a little sooner.

If you visit a gym, fitness center, or if you accidentally walk into a nutritionist's office, chances are you will see what is called a Food Guide Pyramid. This illustration, Figure 2, very simply shows basic recommendations concerning what foods to eat and specifies the range of servings. The top of the pyramid shows fats, oil, and sweets, which are to be eaten sparingly. As you go down the pyramid, the recommended foods include vegetables and fruits. Here, you can eat from two to five servings. The fruit and vegetable group is where you can eat more and ingest less calories. Servings of bread, rice, pasta, and cereals are unrestricted (6 to 11 servings). Eat sparsely of fats, red meats, and oils; and increase your intake of vegetables, fruits, pasta, and cereal grains and your calorie intake will drop. You won't go away hungry, and nutrition levels will be more than satisfied. You're going to continue to crave animal fats, but the craving won't be so hard to overcome.

A healthy weight level is a function of many factors, but food intake and exercise are the primary drivers. Active people need a lot of carbohydrates, so substitution of carbohydrates for fat is a first step in changing that metabolic setpoint. If you are overweight, exercise should be taken in smaller doses. Patience will be a factor; but, after six weeks, you're going to see some good results, that is, if you're consistent with your program. As you progress, the amount of exercise can be increased until at some point you will be at the appropriate healthy level for you. Voilá!

Nutrition

Each person is unique, and your nutritional needs may be somewhat different than others. What we must constantly keep in mind is that nutrition, good or bad, is without question tied to *what and how much* food you put into your mouth. In our discussion on obesity and diet, we covered what and how much food should be eaten to maintain a healthy balance. Further discussion on nutrition for us to better understand the foods we eat and what we can expect to derive from them.

There are many excellent books written on nutrition.[6]

Understanding just the bare basics, which all of us interested folks should do, involves a discussion of carbohydrates, protein, and that old nemesis fat. A knowledge of the basics is all we need in a fitness program, because being calorie smart and knowing what to eat will, along with exercise, keep us competitive and healthy.

An optimum calorie intake is high in carbohydrates and fiber, moderate in protein, and low in fat, cholesterol, salt, alcohol,

---

6. If you wish to go into a more complete presentation on nutrition, the author recommends *Eat, Drink & Be Healthy,* Janet M. Chiavetta, Piedmont Publishers, Raleigh, NC, 1992.

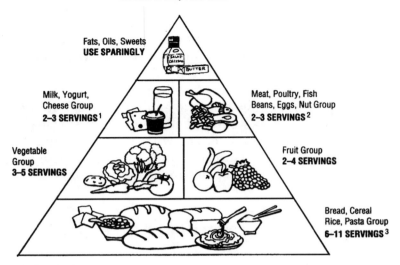

[1] One serving equals 1 cup or 1 ounce cheese. Use skim or low-fat dairy products. Adult men and women over 25 years old require 2 servings/day (except for women who are pregnant, nursing or over 50 years.) The recommendation for children up to 9 years is 2–3 servings/day; for children 9 to 12 years, 3–4 servings/day; for ages 12 to 24 and pregnant women, 3 to 4 servings/day; for nursing mothers, 4 servings per day; and for women over 50 years, 3–5 servings/day.

[2] In order to minimize saturated fat and cholesterol, eat more beans and less meat. To limit fat to 20% of total calories, eat *a maximum of:*

- 3–4 oz. cooked lean meat, poultry, shrimp, crab or lobster or
- 4–6 oz. cooked fish, clams, scallops and oysters

plus, eat *an average of:*

- 1/2 to 3/4 cup beans per day. (Use nuts sparingly.)

Eggs should be limited to no more than 4 per week from all sources, including baked goods and sauces. If you have elevated cholesterol, it is preferable to use egg substitutes or egg whites, which can be consumed in unlimited quantities.

[3] Include at least 2 to 4 servings of whole grain foods.

Figure 2. Food Guide Pyramid
Adapted from: U.S. Department of Agriculture

and caffeine. First, we must determine what our individual calorie intake should be. The approximate calorie intake for a woman 60 and over is about 1800 calories per day; for a man 60 and over, 2400 calories per day is about right.

Another way to approximate your daily calorie needs is to compute it as follows:

1. If you are moderately active, multiply your weight by a number between 15 and 18.
2. If you are very active, multiply your weight by 18.

Obviously, the values obtained are approximate as individual nutritional needs vary. However, the general guidelines cited should be followed, and radical departures from the values should only be made by your doctor or nutritionist. If you wish to be much more accurate, you can visit a nutritionist who will have you record everything you eat and drink over a period of time. Based on your activity level, a calorie intake based on your specific needs will then be determined.

How fast should a dieter lose weight? A good general guideline to follow is: a man should not lose more than two pounds each week, and a woman not more than one pound each week. Refer to published weight charts to determine what your ideal weight should be. Rapid weight loss is often related to water weight loss because of exercise. Losing weight too quickly is simply not a good way to reduce.

The real world we live in, not being perfect (often not even close), will provide us with challenges requiring some common sense on our part. For example, at social gatherings you cannot always eat what fits in with your nutritional needs. A dietary regimen needs flexibility, and occasionally eating something not acceptable can be condoned. Don't give up camaraderie with family and friends by being too rigid! Just be as careful as you can during those friendly parties, and if you won't eat certain taboo items, those who are with you will show a surprising understanding. Social get-togethers add joy to life and offer you a wonderful opportunity to quietly set a good example.

It should be noted that Americans are not the best fed (nutritionally) people in the world. Deficiencies are measured in terms of minerals, vitamins, and protein. But, unfortunately Americans suffer from excesses, e.g., malnutrition caused by too much fat, too much cholesterol, too much caffeine, and too much alcohol. It's ironic that our malnutrition is due to excesses rather than deprivation.

Smoking, long known as a physiological disaster, is becoming more prevalent among our young. It would be of little advantage here to discuss the tragedy of smoking, its harmful cardiovascular effects, and alcohol—both of which create dependency problems. Neither have a place in sustaining a degree of good health. Our efforts here are not to lecture about such well-known detriments to health, but to inform and impart knowledge gained from research and experience (good and bad) to those willing to improve their well being.

Before getting into the specifics of nutrition, it is prudent to discuss the importance of water. Water is critical to your biochemistry. Dehydration, the loss of water in the body, reduces the volume of blood. This causes the blood to become thicker and stresses the heart. As a result, less oxygen and nutrients are available to the muscles.

Approximately 85 percent of our body weight is made up of water. This level is necessary to support its chemistry. One percent fluid loss causes your body to become dehydrated. And you cannot depend on your thirst to tell you when dehydration is happening. When you become thirsty in an endurance event, you are already too low on water and your performance will already be reduced. Dehydration is a common cause of poor athletic performance, which is in part because muscles have a limited capacity to store water.[7]

In any discussion on nutrition, with regard to any corrections to be made, we must emphasize that fat is usually the culprit. In Western countries, the majority of the people live on a diet of which 40 percent of the calories come from fat. Remember,

7. Robert C. Cooper, *Health & Fitness Excellence,* Houghton Mifflin, Boston, 1989, pp. 254–255.

earlier on, we concluded that a healthy balance involved a 65, 20, and 15 percent carbohydrate, fat, and protein balance. Is that enough to sustain a competitive, over-fifty athlete? The answer is probably "yes," as long as we adapt our calorie intake to suit our energy needs.

It doesn't take a space scientist to understand that a 40 percent fat diet is not only too high, but such a diet will be robbing us of needed carbohydrates and protein. Cutting back to an intake of 20 percent of calories from fat will result in a weight loss, if you remain physically active. You can expect to improve your performance by being calorie smart.

Carbohydrates. Eating the proper amount of fruits, vegetables, and grains provides the carbohydrates your body needs. Carbohydrates provide a supply of vitamins, minerals, and fiber to your body. Maintaining a calorie intake at 65 percent of your total daily amount in conjunction with the recommended 15 percent protein intake reduces the amount of fat consumed. A diet rich in carbohydrates provides health benefits including reducing the risk of heart disease and cancer.

A large amount of the energy used up during physical exercise comes from carbohydrates. To support an adequate level, the U.S. Department of Agriculture recommends that we eat three to five servings of vegetables per day and two to four servings of fruit (consider a serving as half a cup). It is best to vary the fruits and vegetables you eat to ensure that you get sufficient amounts of vitamins C and A, and fiber.

There is a misconception that starches are fattening. Actually, starches such as potatoes and pasta are fairly low in calories, unless you add rich gravies or sauces to them. Potatoes (rich in potassium) and pasta are great sources of carbohydrates.

Vegetables, fruits, rice, wheat grains, corn products, barley, rye, oats, and beans are all excellent sources of carbohydrates. These foods can be prepared in many ways, so it's easy to include them in your diet. Although some of these foods may not meet your tastes, there is such an abundance of them that plenty of other choices are available.

Fat. The number of calories of fat recommended by many leading nutritionists is 20 percent of your daily intake. No more saturated fat than 7 percent of your daily intake should be consumed. Medical authorities favor this restriction of saturated fat as a means to reduce cholesterol levels to below 200mg/dl. The restriction of saturated fat and cholesterol reduces the risk of heart disease and cancer. The overall limit of total fat intake is essential in combating obesity.

A daily intake of 20 percent is an achievable goal. An average of 40 percent of the American people's total daily calorie consumption is made up of fat. This amount is far too much, since an adult's daily requirement can be met by an intake of about 10 percent from all sources, e.g., the various foods we eat.

Let's consider that an average person cuts back from a 40 percent fat intake to 20 percent. For a 2500 calorie diet, the 20 percent reduction amounts to 500 calories. Dividing 500 by 9 (calories per gram of fat) equals a reduction of 56 grams of fat. Replacing the 56 grams with carbohydrates and protein equals 56 times 4 (calories per gram of carbos and protein), or 224 calories. By switching to carbohydrates and protein you have reduced calorie intake by 500 minus 224 for a reduction of 276 calories. And you have taken in the same amount of food by weight! This sample calculation assumes that your normal activity has remained the same.

The fat and oil we consume consists of saturated, polyunsaturated, and mono-unsaturated fats. Very simply, saturated fats are solid at room temperature, similar to the fat you see in red meat. Polyunsaturated fats are more liquid at room temperature and will turn rancid or spoil more quickly. Mono-unsaturated fats have a different chemical structure than polyunsaturated fats, are more liquid, and have an even shorter shelf life.

Substituting polyunsaturated and mono-unsaturated fats for saturated fat has the benefit of reducing cholesterol. However, both polyunsaturated and mono-unsaturated fats do contain some saturated fat. The best policy is to use mono-unsaturated fats whenever possible. A substantial reduction in saturated fat can be achieved by using low-fat margarine and preparing foods with olive oil, sunflower oil, safflower oil, and—best of all—canola oil.

It is interesting to note that fat and oils represent 44 percent of the fat consumption in the American diet. Red meats make up about 30 percent; dairy products and eggs comprise 14 percent, and grain, beans, poultry, and fish make up the remaining 12 percent.[8]

There are some obvious corrections that can be made to reduce fat intake. Substituting oils lower in saturated fat for highly saturated oils can make a big dent. The big advantage is that this trade-off does not affect taste or the amount of food to be eaten. Using low-fat margarine instead of butter and reducing the consumption of red meat to once or twice a week will also help. While it will take some getting used to, substituting skim milk for whole milk will make a substantial difference. Now, about that sausage and bacon for breakfast—forget them, and eat more wholesome cereal.

If you follow these simple guidelines, you won't have to calculate each value in calories and fat for the foods you eat. It helps to read the nutrition labels on any food you buy (and in particular those you think might be taboo items). The newer labels are not that hard to understand. It used to be that you couldn't always believe labels that stated, "low fat," or "lite." But new rules enforced by the Food and Drug Administration require specific meanings concerning terms used by food manufacturers. Some of the important terms and their corresponding meanings are as follows:

Fat Free: Less than 0.5 grams of fat per serving.

Low Fat: 3 grams of fat (or less) per serving.

Lean: Less than 10 grams of fat, 4.5 grams of saturated fat, and no more than 95 milligrams of cholesterol per serving.

Light (Lite): 1/2 less calories or no more than 1/2 the fat of the higher-calorie, higher-fat version; or no more than 1/2 the sodium of the higher-sodium version.

Cholesterol Free: Less than 2 milligrams of cholesterol and 2 grams (or less) of saturated fat per serving.

It will be to your advantage to spend a little time reading

---

8. Janet M. Chiavetta, *Eat, Drink & Be Healthy*. Piedmont Publications, Raleigh, NC, 1992, p. 33.

and understanding the labels. You may even want to count your calorie intake for a few days to determine what your calorie consumption is. If you are obese and you find that your weight is coming down after about six weeks, if you feel good and are not tired all of the time, then you can assume that you are on the right track. All that counting may then seem somewhat academic. A program that combines exercise and good nutritional control should be kept simple. Be your own judge on how much counting you want to do. It is important to determine if you are progressing toward your fitness goals. And forget about going to Kenya; you can trim down here and not have to live in some remote hut. Besides, you won't have to run without shoes.

Some of us like to keep lots of records and count calories, fat, carbohydrates, protein, sodium, and that bad cholesterol. That extra work will add some preciseness to your program. These people just like to be very thorough. A list of many foods can be found in the back of this book. The list and the food labels should give most or all of the information you need.

Protein. Protein is an essential part of our diet. It is needed to build muscles, tendons, ligaments, hair, and nails. It is necessary to maintain a proper fluid balance, which is very important to the aspiring as well as the veteran athlete. Protein is also needed to produce enzymes, hormones, and antibodies among other things, which are too technical to discuss here. Protein should make up a maximum of 15 percent of our diet. Although protein is vitally important, too much may not be beneficial. This is a situation similar to the amount of fat recommended—more is not better. Children and pregnant women will need more to aid in the growth of additional body tissue.

Adequate protein levels can be achieved without eating meat, fish, and poultry every day. Obviously, we try to cut down on these items to reduce our fat intake. Beans and grains are excellent sources of protein. Vegetables, bread, white and brown rice, skim milk, and eggs are food products that will give you generous amounts of protein. As you may notice, you also get your intake of carbohydrates from most of these same foods.

A healthy, active life style supplemented by an adequate diet will take care of your vitamin, mineral, and fiber needs. To do this, vary the protein-producing foods you eat. It is not considered essential to take additional vitamins and minerals other than what you get from the foods you eat. Vitamin A, vitamin B6, vitamin C, calcium, iron, and magnesium are the elements most often found lacking in the American diet. However, varying the fruits, vegetables, grains, etc., you eat will help you maintain a nutritional balance. Refer to the charts in the back of the book for the amount of protein in the foods of your choice.

Sodium. There has been some disagreement about the amount of salt our bodies require. Some coaches have recommended that more salt is needed for the athlete, especially during hot weather. The Recommended Dietary Allowance (RDA) for sodium is a maximum of 2400 milligrams per day. That's slightly more than 1 teaspoon of salt. Experts say our bodies need only 500 milligrams per day. That's not much, and it is an unrealistic goal to meet. Major changes will be required by most of us just to maintain the 2400 milligram daily level.

The problem with sodium intake is that most of it does *not* come from the salt shaker. About 30 to 40 percent of the salt comes from the salt shaker and from that used in cooking. Only 10 percent comes naturally from the foods we eat. The largest amount comes from processed foods, with about 10 percent coming from breads, grains, and cereals.[9] So, keep the sodium consumption down to the recommended level established by the RDA. We must be very careful; very little should come from the salt shaker. That's tough for most of us, because salt is a major flavor enhancer, and it is a required ingredient in bread. Sauces have a lot of salt and should be used in moderation. Canned soups are loaded with salt, and, of course, popcorn, potato chips, and fat foods are too, except some brands are now available that have a low-salt content.

It's easy to add up the salt you use by reading the labels. You will be surprised at how much salt is in some of the products we

---

9. Janet M. Chiavetta, *Eat, Drink & Be Healthy,* Piedmont Publishers, Raleigh, NC, 1992, p. 61.

eat, and you will find restricting the amount of salt is going to be a challenge. But, hang in there, it's not that tough.

Conditioning

Throughout this chapter, a combination of diet and exercise has been emphasized. We know dieting alone will not keep your weight down over the long haul. Suppose, however, that you had the fortitude to get your weight down and to keep it there, without getting into an exercise program. That by itself would be a significant first step only, because your body would not be properly conditioned.

Developing the body into a "conditioned" state requires anaerobic and aerobic exercise. Without exercise, the composition of your body will not be satisfactory. Too much of your weight will be fat, without enough muscle mass. And we are not talking about weight lifting here.

Your ideal weight should consist of a combination of lean weight and fat weight. Exercise will increase your lean weight and reduce the fat. Your lean weight will increase as you approach your ideal weight. An ideal fat percentage for the athlete is 15 percent for men and 22 percent for women.

Fat percentages may be lower for professional athletes and for those participating in the Olympics (including the Senior Olympics). These lower values, often going down to 5 percent, are not recommended for other athletes because of the risk of injury and the lack of a proper nutritional balance. Male competitive swimmers in the lower age groups have fat percentages ranging from 6 to 12 percent, and competitive female swimmers have fat levels ranging from 12 to 18 percent.[10] The risks involved with very low body fat percentages are not worth the effort for those over fifty, because competition for the most part is recreational and not part of our livelihood.

10. Mark Schubert, *Sports Illustrated Competitive Swimming: Techniques for Champions,* Time, Inc., 1990.

Measuring body fat can be easily done using skin-fold calipers found in fitness centers and health clubs. Skin-fold measurements are taken at five positions on the body. These measurements are converted to determine your body fat. Other ways of measuring body fat exist, but the caliper method is reasonably accurate and is easy to do.

A person beginning an exercise program may not experience an immediate change or reduction in body weight. During exercise, those muscles will firm up as you trim down. As you increase muscle mass, and reduce body fat, your weight may increase somewhat. So, don't despair during the first 6 weeks or so. If you are obese, a gradual weight loss will begin if you stay with the program.

When discussing conditioning, it is important to stress that overtraining can be counterproductive. Overtraining and stress can cause the body to lose muscle and accumulate fat. So, any exercise regimen should be conducted using sound judgment. Later chapters on running, swimming, and cycling will establish categories of achievement to guide you. In the meantime, as you trim down, avoid getting overtired and space any exercise routines so your muscles can adapt to the increased activity. Chapter Three will help you get started.

Three
Choices

Goals

Suppose one day after taking a shower you stand in the bathroom and look at yourself in the mirror. You're sixty years old, and you don't like what you see. Your gut is hanging out, you look flabby. If you are a woman viewing yourself, you see hips that are bulging—wow, look at that ugly cellulite! Your breasts sag and your underarm flesh is hanging loosely. As a man, you may look good from the rear, but from the front you see a big gut and lots of flab. You say to yourself, "Better get some clothes on before someone sees me. Maybe something loose would be nice."

The flab and bulges are but the outer appearance of a body out of shape, with very poor muscle tone—and with less muscle mass than should be on that frame. For many, the situation just described, or one similar to it, is a strong signal to enter into some sort of fitness program.

Well, for the sake of presenting an example of how you might get into an exercise program, let's say that you decide to do some walking. So, being logical, you determine that once a week isn't going to do much, and you decide three times a week is an appropriate start. Now being reasonably bright, you get comfortable shoes, and off you go. So far, you've done everything right, except it is very important to talk to your doctor first.

Walking is a good start, because it will improve your cardiovascular condition, tone up those leg muscles, and relieve some stress. A walking program should always precede a running program for the beginner. What this exercise effort *won't* do is reduce all of the flab and bulges. The extra exercise will burn more calories, but your appetite will tend to compensate. That's why Chapter One was presented first, so you could reduce your fat intake. What we are going to tell you throughout this book is that to lose weight you must enter into a program that combines exercise and calorie reduction.

We could have included a lot of low calorie menus. But, you are probably not a chef, and if you have to be bothered with fixing a lot of low-calorie meals, you won't follow through with the program.

Most veteran athletes don't get involved with special meals; they just compensate by not eating a lot of fatty foods, cutting out red meat every day, doing away with bacon and sausage for breakfast, and adding fruits, vegetables, rice, and grains to their diets. These athletes have learned what to avoid, while eating the other good stuff without going hungry.

While doing those walks, you will have plenty of time to think out your program. Your brain is like gravity; it never shuts down, although there are some who will argue that there are lazy folks who have completely sedentary gray matter.

The combination of calorie reduction and exercise will show substantial benefits after about six weeks. Remember, 1 pound of body weight equals 3500 calories. You will see it on the scales and in how you feel; that is, if you made it part of your lifestyle. Excuses never win races and never show anything but poor results!

While thinking during those walks, which seem to get brisker, you begin to get the urge for additional challenge. Maybe you should run a little, get a bike, or do some lap swimming? These are good thoughts, but with exercise it is best to make haste slowly. Let your muscles become conditioned, and make sure your weight is down enough to withstand some running. Running is an impact sport where injuries are common. Biking will place some stress on leg and arm muscles, and swimming will emphasize technique and upper body strength. Each of these endurance sports will be covered later.

An important point to be made here is that you should "listen" to your body. Pain that recurs or does not go away is a signal from your body to stop or at the very least to slow down. A potential injury can come from numerous sources. Overuse is a common source of injury, even with beginners. For example, shoes can be a source of knee injuries, as well as running around the track in the same direction too much. Running downhill may cause hamstring soreness, and charging the hills too hard may cause discomfort in your quadriceps (those big muscles in your front thigh).

After doing some light and easy running without injury, it's time to follow some rules to help you along. Senior runners who compete, especially those in the Senior Olympics, follow them carefully:

a. Before a race, an endurance event, or just a run for a couple of miles, runners and bikers should run or bike for short trial distances to loosen up, and then go through a series of stretching exercises. Swimmers should do a few easy pool lengths in each of the strokes they will use in competition or the strokes on which they will be working. Stretching is good for swimmers too.

b. Always drink lots of water. If you are going to do a long, hard endurance event, it is a good idea to start hydrating a day or two before (when you start making a lot of trips to the bathroom, you will know you are hydrated). During a running or biking event of 5K or more don't pass up any water stops. You will remember we discussed the importance of water in Chapter Two.

c. In endurance events, pace yourself; learn to stay aerobic as discussed in Chapter One.

d. Rest between races or hard workouts. Go hard one day and go easy the next. After races, rest a day or so. Very hard, long races require more than just one day of rest. Always rest completely one day each week.

e. You can go through some discomfort if it goes away as you exercise. This will happen when sore muscles warm up or as you pass from the anaerobic to the aerobic phase. Never try to run through any form of chest pain, even if you think it is just indigestion. Angina, heart-related pain, which may occur in the chest or down the left arm, may disappear as you exercise. You should always stop when any form of chest or arm pain occurs.

f. Stretch and cool down after strenuous exercise. This is an important step often overlooked by many. Proper cool-down will allow the blood concentrated in those large muscles to begin to circulate to your upper body, especially to your brain. Your legs are your heart's best friend. Never sit down immediately after strenuous activity. Cool down slowly by walking after a run or after biking. Swimmers can cool down easily by swimming slowly for half a lap or so. If you don't do it, one hot day you will pass out.

Decisions

We are now in a position to get into the goal setting process. We've walked and started running. Compensations have been made to our diet. All of this has been done without compiling a lot of charts and recording times. We haven't gone through a lot of complicated menus. Good judgment has saved us from injury and made us calorie smart. Results are looking good. Best of all, we are mentally alert, and our bodies feel great. Now, one of two things can happen:

1. You can decide to get competitive and take the necessary steps to do so.
2. You can continue to stay in shape with calorie discretion and exercise.
Either way you win!

Unless you have the desire to be competitive, there is no need to push yourself any harder. You may enter into some local fun runs, bike races, or join the United Masters Swimming organization (local branches have swimming events throughout the year). Have some fun! If you're satisfied with how you look in that bathroom mirror, you have reached your goal. So what if the neighbors appear to be a little jealous? If they say anything, give them a copy of this book.

But, maybe you have awakened that old competitive instinct, and you want to get serious? That's also a viable choice, and suggestions for the serious senior athlete can be found in later chapters.

Four
Running

The 80-year-old had just finished a marathon. We all agreed that it was an outstanding effort—he finished! But, he thought he could have done it faster!

Running to Excel

Your decision to become competitive should not be taken lightly. Training takes time and commitment; you cannot go out and run for a few miles a couple of times a week and expect satisfactory results. Unless you can get your family involved, a beneficial aerobic program will take time away from your family. And if you work for a living, there will be another part of the day from which you cannot take time. So, after your family and job and other priority obligations, you will need to sort out the time that is left for this other priority assignment you have chosen. Then, you need time to *sleep*.

Many Americans walk for fitness—about forty million of them. In countries where only a few own automobiles, walking and bicycling are a way of life. In those countries diets are often high in carbohydrates. We, on the other hand, have to enter into a walking program to get fit. We are lucky in that food is plentiful, and unlucky in that, with so many choices, we often make the wrong selections.

We don't have to go on foot to get to work, so if we walk or run it is outside the scope of what we have to do to earn a living and take care of our family. Therefore, if we are to walk or run, it has to be part of our discretionary time.

Getting Started

For the person who decides to begin running, the best way to start is to begin after a walking program. Dr. Kenneth H. Cooper, who started all this aerobics business in the late 1960s, set a lot of standards for walking/running, cycling, and swimming.[11] In this book, we want to take you through a very simple, achievable program that will also help you to reach endurance goals. You will be surprised how much you can improve and how good you will feel about your accomplishments. But, you must stay the course!

Before beginning a running program, you should be able to walk at a rate of fifteen minutes per mile for three miles. Figure 3 shows how a beginner can progress in a walking program. Walking fifteen-minute miles is not as easy as it may appear. Not all of us are equal, so if you are a little slow, walk another week or so until you get close. Excellent aerobic benefits will require walking fifteen-minute miles for at least thirty minutes, four or five times a week.

As you start running (as you did when you began walking), you will need to pay attention to your running shoes. The shoes you use when walking may be satisfactory for running. However, as you begin running, the impact on your feet, legs, thighs, and knees will increase. You may find that you need a shoe with more cushion and with a better fit. Fitting a runner into a shoe is complex. Find a sports store that employs someone who can fit you properly. You may spend a few extra bucks getting the correct shoe, but you will save money by eliminating medical expenses later.

Getting into running will require you to step up your activity slowly. For example, suppose you can walk three miles in a little less than forty-five minutes. That's stepping along pretty good. Now, you can think about training for competition running. How you start can be accomplished in a number of different ways. Our

---

11. Kenneth H. Cooper, M.D., *The New Aerobics,* New York, M. Evans and Company, Inc., 1970.

WEEK	MIN/MILE	TIME (MIN)	DISTANCE (MI)	FREQ/WK
1	18	15	0.83	3
2	17	15	0.93	3
3	17	20	1.17	3
4	17	30	1.76	3
5	16	30	1.87	4
6	16	40	2.5	4
7 & ON	15	45	3.0	5

Figure 3. Walking Goals

plan here is to present to you a way that will work, and it will work for everyone with a minimum of injury.

First, drink some water; warm up by running easily until you just begin to break a sweat, then stretch; and don't walk or run within two hours after eating. If you are anxious or nervous for any reason, allow more than two hours, since your food will take longer to pass through your stomach. Begin your running program by walking briskly for about a mile, then run slowly for another mile, and finish the third mile walking. Next, cool down. When you cool down, do not stop walking but continue at a slow pace until your heart rate drops; then, walk a bit more and stretch.

You may find that middle 1-mile section a bit difficult at first, or if you are in good condition, it may be easy. Do what you can, and increase the running distance by about 10 percent each week. If any discomfort or pain persists, back off or stop until the injury heals. If you increase your running distance at a modest pace, an injury most likely will not occur. Injuries, however, may occur with some who start out pushing too hard. We will cover injuries later.

It is important to *run slowly at first* so you can build up your endurance. The 3-mile distance is intended to adjust your body to running for longer times. Improving your speed should be accomplished later in your conditioning program.

You should continue increasing your distance until you can run the entire 3-mile distance. Stay with this distance for a couple of weeks until your body catches up by conditioning itself to the increased stress. Now, you can choose to increase your mileage, or run the three miles faster.

The best course would be to increase your running distance by about 10 percent each week until you reach a 6-mile distance. Then, start increasing your speed by slowly increasing your aerobic limit. Remember, this is a running level or speed at which your heart and breathing rate stabilize (does not increase or decrease).

As you push to increase your aerobic limit, be careful to "listen" to your body for any pain that may lead to an injury. Increasing your aerobic limit is the process of running faster for prolonged periods with your heart and breathing rate stabilized. Your body has an aerobic range. At a slower running rate, you will be at a lower aerobic rate, and your breathing will be steady and easy. As you increase your speed, your breathing rate will increase. If your breathing rate stabilizes, you will still be in your aerobic range. As you body condition improves, your aerobic upper limit will increase. Improved or increased aerobic levels will permit you to run faster for longer time periods.

As you speed up to a point where you can no longer stay at a level breathing rate and begin to gasp for air, you will have exceeded the aerobic limit. Pushing this limit (without gasping for air) will increase your running distance until at some point you will reach your peak capability.

The reason for suggesting a 6-mile target is that you will then be in condition to run 90 percent of the local racing events. For events longer than the popular 10K (6.2 miles), you will have to train for longer distances. For the longer distances, including the marathon (26.2 miles), you can use the same training philosophy as prescribed for six miles, except you can't run the long training runs as often, and training refinements to suit your needs and time constraints will have to be developed.

Progress at a slow pace, and pace yourself by staying within your aerobic range. If you exceed your aerobic upper limit (going anaerobic) too often, your muscle fibers will begin to break down, you will be at risk for an injury, and your efficiency will drop off during the later stages of the run.

The great part about racing competition is that you will soon find out how you stand with the rest of the runners in your age group. If you finish in the back of the pack, remember three things:

1. There will always be someone better than you, but, on a given day you may, for various reasons, finish up front.
2. You can go back and train. You weren't going to quit anyway.
3. Those finishing in the back of the pack just might be in the upper (physical) 2 percent of the general population.

Understanding the running program training regimen wasn't too hard, was it? As a caution, the method just described can have many variations, depending on your physical ability and mental outlook. Progress must be made without haste, or without exception you will end up hurt. Those world-class runners didn't get to the top overnight, and most of them ended up getting hurt by pushing their limits beyond what the body would accept.

Of the thousands of seniors running, only a few ever get to compete at the national level. Those few who reach that level have a combination of natural ability, good coaches, perseverance, a little luck, and the time to train properly. Chances are you will never be in that select group, but then no one should say you can't do it, because maybe you can. Whatever, if you're competitive and do your best, you will feel good about it all.

Now, take another look in that mirror!

Stepping Up the Pace. The established runner, one who runs distances up to a 1/2 marathon and an occasional marathon, knows by pacing himself or herself the distance is always achievable (barring illness or unforeseen incidents). Their goals then relate to running the distances faster and improving their personal records (PRs).

There are all kinds of schemes and philosophies for improving those times. The bottom line is that the athlete must continue to stretch his or her aerobic limit using one, or more, or all of the theories that abound. At the end of Chapter One, we proposed some guidelines. These hold true for the veteran or elite runner as well as for the novice.

All runners must rest, because some healing is always required after every run. Likewise, your body needs more food to replenish the energy used up during exercise. We are not revealing deep, dark secrets here; you eat every day to replace the energy you use up. Except, as an athlete, you use up much more energy and place significantly more stress on those muscles.

How you conduct your training and how often you can push to your limit should be carefully thought out. Watch those accomplished and experienced runners and talk to them to find out how they train. Try to follow what they do within your capability, but stay within those guidelines.

Figure 4 is an example of a 7-day training schedule and may be followed after having reached the 6-mile limit prescribed earlier.

The schedule and goals in Figure 4 are examples of how runners might train. The mileage relates to older runners, and if pain occurs or you become very tired, back off on the miles. Older runners should not maintain the training intensity of younger runners because older folks heal slower, and more rest is needed. Long distance runners run more miles, but three to five miles on a given day is more than satisfactory for those who compete in 10K distances or shorter.

If you decide to run a 1/2 marathon or a marathon, you will need to increase your mileage and add an additional rest day. Usually, clinics are held well in advance of the long runs. Attend those clinics if you can, and pick up helpful advice. We recommend at least fourteen weeks of distance training for a marathon, which applies only to those already involved with the shorter distances.

One endurance event should not have value over another. Shorter races are as difficult as the longer events. Longer events require excellent pacing and the discomfort of running lasts a longer time. Going through the long endurance test is also an exercise in mental strength. The short 3K (1.8 miles) race can be lost by going out too fast and dropping down to the anaerobic level too often. So the shorter runs can be just as difficult as the longer, except the time is shorter. The intensity of discomfort may be greater, because the athlete will try to stay at his or her highest possible aerobic level.

Warm-Ups and Cool-Downs. Warm-ups and cool-downs should always be conducted before and after every race or practice session. They will help you not only to avoid injury, but will also decrease the discomfort that occurs one or two days after a difficult race. Each race stretches the muscle fibers and often tears them slightly. The muscles need time to heal, so it is imperative to get rest after a hard run or race.

When you warm up, the muscle fibers get warm and become

Category I - Beginners

DAY	TRAINING LEVEL
Monday	Run 4 to 5 miles hard
Tuesday	Run 3 to 4 miles easy
Wednesday	Run 4 to 5 miles hard
Thursday	Run 3 miles or rest
Friday	Run hills, try to go for 5 miles w/level stretches in between
Saturday	Run 5 miles easy
Sunday	Rest and spoil your family

Category II - Serious Runners

DAY	TRAINING LEVEL
Monday	Run 5 to 7 miles hard
Tuesday	Run 4 to 5 miles easy
Wednesday	Run 4 to 5 miles hard
Thursday	Run 4 miles easy or rest
Friday	Run hills, try to go for 5 miles w/level stretches in between
Saturday	Run 6 miles easy
Sunday	Watch a sports event with your family

Figure 4. Running Goals

softer and more pliable. As these fibers warm, they are able to more easily use up the fuel and oxygen they need. Warming avoids sudden energy needs allowing the heart rate and the metabolic process to gradually increase. Warm-ups also help to lubricate those old aching joints, permitting them to move more freely.

During a race or a training session, your heart pumps at a higher rate, and the blood vessels in your legs dilate. This process forces the blood to the leg muscles providing the needed oxygen necessary to metabolize the energy (from that food you ate) required to pump those legs. As you finish the event, a large amount of your blood is concentrated in the lower part of your body, and you must cool down slowly to let the blood supply return to normal levels in the upper part of your body. If you stop abruptly, the supply of blood to your brain may be diminished enough to cause you to pass out. Cooling down is always important, but in hot weather, it becomes more essential.

Weather

Very few running events are canceled because of the weather. Races are not run in the snow or on icy streets, but many events are started with the runners shivering from the cold and/or the rain. After the start, the discomfort soon goes away when the body heats up, even though a pleasant comfort level may not be achieved until the runner is in the shower and thinking about relaxing in the reclining chair.

Runners are a hardy lot. It seems that very few choose not to run because of bad weather. Occasionally, an event will start at a temperature as low as 10° F. Keeping warm until the starting gun goes off, is accomplished in various ways and is left to the wiles of the runner. Gloves and hoods are used, but often the hoods disappear when the runner is well into the race. The gloves have to stay on, however, when temperatures are below freezing. Mittens seem to keep the hands warmer than gloves.

Kudos are due to those who endure the rigors of cold and otherwise bad weather. Not many who participate ever complain about conditions, for they have come to compete. It is that way for almost all of the senior adult sporting events, regardless of the type of sport. Sports is their way to continue on with life in a healthy, fit way. Why complain about that?

Heat is another matter. No event or training session should be conducted in temperatures over 90° F. Unfortunately, some events occur at elevated temperatures. As the temperature increases late in spring, it is necessary for runners to train as the temperatures begin to rise. The body will gradually begin to adapt to the higher temperatures, but there is a limit, which is different for each of us.

Runners competing in a climate different than that in which they have trained should train in the new climate prior to competing. To achieve maximum performance, it is necessary for the body to adapt to changes in wind, heat, cold, and altitude conditions. It is more difficult to perform at high humidities, and the competitor should use common sense and not train or compete at low wind-chill levels.

Heat exhaustion and heat stroke are serious conditions that any runner, young or old, must recognize. Both are physical failures of the body to cope with and compensate for elevated heat conditions; heat stroke is the most serious. It would be unwise to ignore or make light of either of these two possible problems.

Heat exhaustion is caused by dehydration and the loss of electrolytes. As heat exhaustion develops, your cooling system is on overtime, and you are beginning to sweat heavily. Then, you become dizzy and light-headed. Your skin feels cool and clammy, your salt and potassium become depleted, and you begin to experience muscle cramps. Stop when any of these symptoms occur, find a cool place, drink plenty of water, and rest. Don't wait too long or you will have to go to the hospital for intravenous feeding to replace electrolytes.

Heat stroke is a medical emergency. Heat stroke happens when all of the heat mechanisms within the body have failed, and the body temperature has risen to a point where the brain's regulating mechanism has ceased to function. The body temperature may go as high as 107° to 109° F. Symptoms are: red, hot skin; lack of sweating; and usually, loss of consciousness. Emergency treatment will be needed at once, where an ice bath, ice packs, and a cooling blanket will be used to lower the body temperature.[12] Heat stroke may be fatal. The slightest indication of hot skin or lack of sweating at elevated temperatures make it essential to stop and get cool.

Heat problems can be prevented by checking the temperature and humidity before training or racing. You will usually know from past experience if it's too hot and humid for you; and if there is any doubt, postpone any vigorous activity. It is prudent during hot, humid weather to keep your water intake up. Don't wait until you are thirsty; hydrate early. Don't take salt tablets. Adequate levels of salt are maintained by a proper diet.

As a final precaution, never enter a race under adverse weather conditions where medical aid is not provided. Well organized races provide EMT services at the end of the course, and volunteers cruise the course in vans to locate any athlete having difficulty.

Competition

Competition is fierce, fun, and friendly. After the beginning of a race as the runners in a crowded field were less than a hundred yards from the starting line, a runner stumbled and began to fall. He never reached the ground, because he was pulled up by runners on both sides. He barely lost a step. Most of us run to win, but never is winning so important that we lose compassion for others. It's fun because we can share experiences, compare times for the various events, discuss various training concepts, and we barely notice the cold rain when it is falling!

Choosing the races you want to run is a matter of preference. Some like the longer events; some prefer the shorter distances. Many, who like the shorter sprints and runs, will run the longer events, when the shorter events are not available. It makes for a

12. Allen M. Levy, M.D. and Mark L. Forest, *Sports Injury Handbook: Professional Advice for Amateur Athletes,* John Wiley and Sons, Inc., 1993.

good mix, creating a more well-rounded athlete. Training is essential for either the longer or shorter distances. It's a little difficult to adjust your body to be good at both, although some few do remarkably well.

To be good at either long or short distances, you must train for one or the other. Some will argue this point, but there are few exceptions. Very short distances such as the 100, 400, and 800 meter races will require you to increase your anaerobic ability; so, that is what you must adapt your body to do. Your aerobic ability must be pushed to higher levels as you train for the long races. Longer races require you to train for endurance and speed.

All of this is not to say that you can't compete in races up to a marathon. More than likely, if you train as described in this chapter, you will do well in all races up to the 10,000 meter race. The 1/2 marathon and marathon will require much longer training distances and about fourteen weeks of serious training. For some, competing in the marathon is the ultimate achievement; for others, winning the 400-meter dash is the greatest. It's up to you.

The best place to find out where and when races are to be held in your community is to visit local sporting goods stores or fitness centers. Running clubs exist in many parts of the country. Community centers in the larger metropolitan areas may also be able to provide you with information about upcoming events.

After competing in some events, you may be included on some of the various mailing lists maintained by organizations conducting running events each year. Word of mouth between runners will also alert you to events, often those held out of town or away from the area in which you live. Once you get acquainted, you may find that there are so many races that you won't be able to compete in all of them.

Five
Swimming

I asked this seventy-two-year-old lady, who does the 100 yard breaststroke in 1:34, when she thinks she will slow down, and she said, "I'm not ready yet!"

Swimming and Competing

Swimming is a sport that requires technique, coordination, and upper body strength. Excellence in all three qualities is found in good swimmers. Aerobic conditioning in swimming is achieved in the same way as with running. It takes about 20 minutes of continuous swimming, at least three or four times a week for aerobic fitness. If you are at an excellent aerobic fitness level because of running or biking, you must do some extra upper body conditioning to become a good swimmer.

Most swimmers training for competition are basically fit. They train for distances from 50 yards (or meters) to 5 kilometers and one hour postals.[13] However, many do not have access to a pool often enough to meet their potential. For those swimmers to excel, it is necessary to turn to other forms of exercise to get in top condition. However, in this chapter, we will proceed as if you had access to a training or lap swimming pool for at least three times each week.

Aerobic conditioning is as essential for swimmers as it is for runners and bikers. A runner in good aerobic condition should be

---

13. A one hour postal is a competitive event where a swimmer swims the maximum distance he or she can in one hour.

able to traverse one and a half miles in twelve to thirteen minutes. This will be a positive indication that the lungs, heart, and cardiovascular systems are in good shape. Later we will present some values to determine your swimming capability. A competitive swimmer must train for aerobic capability by lap swimming, although being a good runner won't hurt. During lap swimming, the swimmer must constantly strive to improve technique and coordination.

Any swimming event requiring more than two to three minutes will require the swimmer to develop aerobically. Most swimmers entering competition will swim long distance events as well as the short races. Before determining some goals, it is necessary to establish an aerobic swimming fitness level. It is more complicated to do this for swimmers because of the different strokes involved.

To do all of this well, it is helpful for the swimmer to get instruction from a qualified coach or someone who knows the basic techniques. Without a competent advisor, the essence of that almost perfect stroke may be lost, and the swimmer may be accumulating a lot of mileage without anything but aerobic benefit. In fact, technique and coordination may be so poor and swimming efficiency so low that, during the swim, the swimmer may keep dropping back to the anaerobic phase. As you do lap swimming, you will notice that some swimmers stop for breathers at the end of most laps. Guess what—some of them keep running out of gas because their stroke is so bad that they can't stay in the aerobic phase (some, however, may be doing sprints and taking rests in between).

Conditioning. Because the anaerobic and aerobic energy levels described in Chapter One will also occur in swimming, swimming smart will require you to pace yourself through an endurance event to achieve your maximum potential. Short distances will enhance the anaerobic system capacity. Faster swimmers never get aerobic in events of two or three minutes or less.

The aerobic conditioning that you acquire through lap swimming will build up that muscle tone, and after a time, you will start looking good—to yourself—and others too. Swimming does wonders for the upper body. Of course, for the shorter events and the longer distances too, you will need to practice sprints to improve your speed. It's very similar to a running program.

Swimmers can get by with more weight than those in other sports (a little extra buoyancy doesn't hurt). Nevertheless, prime condition is essential to get to higher levels. But, skinny swimmers do well too. A record holder in the backstroke in the 80 and over category is tall and skinny. The only records he breaks are his own.

Four strokes are used in swimming competition: the crawl or freestyle, the breaststroke, the backstroke, and the butterfly. For most of us, the butterfly is the most difficult. Freestyle is used for the longer distance events, because it is the easiest, most efficient, and the fastest.

It is surprising how many fit persons have difficulty swimming just 200 yards. This is because technique and coordination are such important parts of the sport. It has been estimated that only 2 percent of the population can swim 500 continuous yards. An outstanding fifty-year-old athlete who has not done any lap swimming since high school or college, might have great difficulty doing a 200-yard freestyle swim without a rest between laps. Triathletes, who often begin as runners, soon find that swimming technique becomes vitally important even though they have excellent aerobic endurance capability.

Each of the sports: running, biking, and swimming, require anaerobic and aerobic capability, but not all of the same muscles are used. Therefore, you must work the appropriate muscles and muscle groups pushing them to anaerobic and aerobic limits just like that guy in ancient Greece did with the bull. But, he was an example of anaerobic ability; he couldn't swim and he couldn't run very well.

In swimming, you will need strength as well as technique and coordination. As you swim and train in the different strokes, it will be in your best interest to concentrate on each of the stroke requirements. You will find yourself improving as you build up lap time in each of the strokes. Swimming will take a lot of work—most of it enjoyable. So, don't be too serious, just be stubborn enough to do it, and smart enough to do it right.

Some Standards and Preliminary Goals. For the beginning swimmer or for the swimmer getting back into the pool after many years, it is advisable to set some goals. The goals or standards presented here are for swimmers fifty years old and older and are based on the freestyle or crawl stroke. The broad categories are adaptable for those potential senior Olympians, since beginning in 1996 the limit for participants was lowered to 50. And, would you believe it, many in their forties cannot wait until they are fifty, because now there is a place for them to compete.

The goals are based on categories of achievement rather than by age groups. So, regardless of your age, you can start at a category you think you can handle. Then, as you become better, you can proceed to the higher categories. See Figure 5 for the goals. It would be better for you to choose a level somewhat below what you think you can do. Then, you can go higher without having to back off. You should do some practice swimming to adjust your muscles to the sport before beginning or selecting a category. It will take two to three weeks to aerobically adapt to a new swimming stroke.

When you find the category that suits you, swim through the distances and check your times. If you are a bit slow, try again on your next swim. Fitness and improvement take time! Select a pace you can handle and then progress from week-to-week. Getting through the categories will get you in swimming condition. It will be a good start toward going into competition.

Swimming is a complex sport because of the different strokes. Each stroke has specific techniques that must be learned. You will need to do them so well that you can do them by rote or instinct.

Accordingly, a good coach or friend who is familiar with the different strokes will be very helpful, for a non-competitor can spot the mistakes you make easier than you can. You will soon agree that just getting aerobic or going the distance is not enough. Improvement will require developing your technique and coordination as well. And, then, your speed will improve. You will need to train consistently to progress from one category to the next higher category shown in Figure 5.

YARDS

	BEGINNERS	CATEGORY I	CATEGORY II	CATEGORY III
Distance	Wks 1 thru 5	Wks 1 thru 5	Wks 1 thru 10	As Required
Yards	Time Min/Sec	Time Min/Sec	Time Min/Sec	Time Min/Sec
50	1:00	0:55	0:40	0:30
100	2:10	1:50	1:20	1:09
200	5:10	4:30	3:40	2:38
400	11:10	9:42	8:03	5:45
500	14:15	12:20	10:15	7:19
1000		25:20	21:12	15:07

METERS

	BEGINNERS	CATEGORY I	CATEGORY II	CATEGORY III
Distance	Wks 1 thru 5	Wks 1 thru 5	Wks 1 thru 10	As Required
Meters	Time Min/Sec	Time Min/Sec	Time Min/Sec	Time Min/Sec
50	1:06	1:00	0:43	0:33
100	2:44	2:00	1:28	1:16
200	5:39	4:55	4:06	2:53
400	12:13	10:37	8:49	6:17
500	15:35	13:29	12:19	8:00
1000		27:43	23:11	16:32
1650				

ONE HOUR POSTAL
YARDS   MEN   WOMEN

	CATEGORY I		CATEGORY II		CATEGORY III	
Distance Yards	2050(M)	1880(W)	3650(M)	3150(W)	4350(M)	3640(W)

Figure 5. Swimming Goals

Figure 6 has been prepared to show how aerobic capability will stay with you for long periods of time, provided you stay in excellent shape. This chart shows the actual performance levels that can be expected for various categories of swimmers. Note that the curve does not bend upward (indicating a slower rate) as the distance increases. This is evidence that a fit swimmer slows down very little over the long distance. Any slowing down may actually be psychological, because at the longer distances, the swimmer may feel that he or she is getting tired and should be swimming slower. Or, there is always the fear that maybe the swimmer will get so tired that he or she won't make it to the finish.

The aerobic curve, taken from St. Louis Masters Swimmers events, shows that speed can be maintained over long distances as long as we don't exceed the aerobic limit. Remember, the upper aerobic limit or threshold is that level of fitness activity where you cannot sustain a consistent or even breathing rate. When you exceed your aerobic limit, you will feel discomfort in your arms as your lactic acid builds up. One might ask, "Well, sooner or later the swimmer will slow down from exhaustion. Isn't that true?" The answer is yes. But, that won't happen in long endurance events if you are physically and aerobically fit.

The curve in Figure 6 will begin to grow steeper as the lactic acid begins to build up and you have used up the energy stored in your body. The energy provided by stored carbohydrates is important for maximum performance. The amazing fact is that your body will sustain you through long periods without let-up. It's like a car. Its speed won't change as long as there is gas in the tank, except the body is a much more elegant creation.

One important fact must be stressed before we get into the four different strokes. You should not train at your aerobic limit. It's alright to push the limit once in a while to determine your competitive speed. However, most of your training should be done at 85 percent of your aerobic limit. You will not have much trouble finding your aerobic limit, but you will have to guess how hard you will have to swim to be at the 85 percent limit or somewhat below. An inexpensive heart rate monitor will help you to make a more accurate determination.

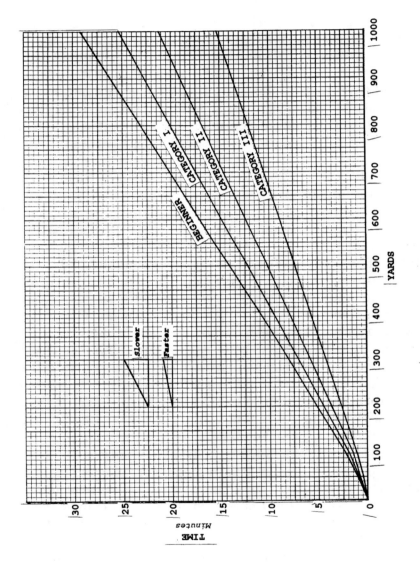

Figure 6. The Aerobic Curve
(Short Course)

The Crawl or Freestyle Stroke. Most of us learned this stroke when we were kids. It is the most efficient, and it was what we learned first, except maybe for the dog paddle. Unless you swam competitively in high school or college, it is likely that for you this first stroke may leave a lot to be desired. Regardless, most of us who begin again after a long layoff need to get back to the basics.

You decide to become fit through swimming, and with a firm resolve, you head down to the local YMCA or recreational pool to swim some laps. If you easily meet the broad "beginning" goals shown in Figure 5, you may soon get back into competition. But, if you have had no formal training, it would be wise to progressively try and meet the goals set forth in Figure 5. Start at a point or level you can meet; then, if you still have difficulty, it will be necessary for you to go through some of the basics and practice, practice, practice. Basics are for all of us—good swimmers or not.

Many of us who return to swimming with bad form will find that others swim by us almost effortlessly, while we struggle to keep up. The crawl is a very efficient stroke (only for humans; dolphins do it without arms or legs), but to get the maximum benefit, we must do it correctly. That soon becomes evident to triathletes and others who often start out as runners. They must complement their excellent running and biking endurance by improving their distance swimming. Developing the proper stroke techniques will enhance their speed, which in competition is very important.

Freestyle Rules. Very few rules apply to the freestyle stroke; any of the four strokes may be used. However, almost without exception the crawl stroke is used, because it is faster. The only rule that applies is that you must touch the end of the pool as you make the turn. You do not have to touch with your hand. Touching with your feet as you push off is satisfactory.

Getting Slippery. Speed is directly related to the position of your body as you travel through the water. Your head should remain half submerged as you swim. Lifting your head will cause your legs and hips to drop down in the water, creating an unnecessary drag or resistance. The longitudinal or lengthwise axis of your body should remain almost parallel to the water surface. Your feet should just break the water as you kick. Of all the corrections to be made, these are probably the most easy to attain.

The Stroke. Terry Laughlin, who teaches efficient swimming, states that many Masters and fitness swimmers believe that an efficient stroke is a prize reserved for the few who won the genetic lottery or spent most of their waking adolescent hours grooming it.[14] He emphasizes that this theory is not true, because the almost perfect stroke can be learned at any age.

If you have a very poor swimming stroke, it will be difficult to change those old habits. One way to change poor techniques, is to concentrate on one part of the stroke at a time, until it becomes a habit. Changing to a good stroke will take lots of practice. But, the results will be well worth the effort.

Excellent swimmers do not always have the fastest stroke rate. Does that surprise you? Often, an increased stroke rate results in a waste of energy. You may disagree after watching the swimmers in the Olympic games. However, if you were to count the number of strokes of the faster swimmers, you would find that they take less strokes per pool length than the slower swimmers. Stroke rate will be discussed later.

Some contend that slippery swimming is the main factor with the winners, and without a doubt, it is an important factor. The actual stroke technique is, however, vital to top-rated swimmers. Without that almost perfect stroke, the swimmer will almost always be in the back of the pack.

It is difficult to describe a swimming stroke in words, but a few good points should be made. Let's start with the stroke just before your hand enters the water. Your arm should be extended forward from the shoulder, just a few inches from being fully extended. Your hand should enter the water at a 45° angle, palm to the outside. As you pull through the stroke, your elbow should remain up, and your arm should form a 90° angle about half way through. At the beginning of the stroke, your hand should move slightly inward and then outward as it passes your hip. The

---

14. Terry Laughlin, "The Slippery Swimmer," *Swim Magazine,* Jul/Aug '96.

stroke should continue rearward until your arm straightens out. Your hand should then leave the water, little pinky first. Experts promote a long follow-through, because the maximum power of the stroke is in the last 1/3 of the stroke.

As your arm and hand leave the water, keep your elbow up without trying to push it up too high. Your hand should just clear the water as you reach forward. As one arm leaves the water for the recovery, the other hand and arm will begin the pull stroke.

Next, is a technique that may be helpful. As your arm reaches to the point where your hand is about to make re-entry, your other arm is stretched forward from the shoulder to begin its stroke. This delayed action, which occurs when both hands are in the forward position, makes maximum use of glide in the water. Some older swimmers use this technique, since the glide helps them to save energy for a more powerful stroke. More powerful strokes mean less strokes for each length of the pool you travel, regardless of the method. As you practice your stroke, allow your body to rotate about 45° as you reach forward to make the stroke.[15]

Hands. Those hands! What about those hands? Most of us have been taught to cup our hands through the power pull of the stroke. Some coaches contend that whether your hand is cupped or held flat, or whether your fingers are open or closed is not important. Some very good swimmers swim with their fingers slightly open. We suggest swimming with your fingers together.

Strength. Strength is always an important factor. Who can argue that a more powerful stroke will not result in more distance per stroke? Not all of us are genetically blessed with an abundance of upper body strength. Some good swimmers do very well without a hefty upper torso, because of exceptional technique, coordination, and a powerful kick. However, upper body strength can be developed through weight training. It can be accomplished in the gym, and it will improve as you continue to

---

15. For a thorough and comprehensive technical description of the swimming strokes, we recommend *Swimming Faster,* by Ernest W. Maglischo, Mayfield Publishing Company, 1982.

swim. If a fitness center or a gym is available to you, ask the instructor to demonstrate what exercises will help. As you accumulate swimming distance, the specific muscles used for the stroke you are using will tone up.

Stroke Rate. It is difficult to tell swimmers what their stroke rate should be. As a general rule, the stroke rate can be increased as long as you maintain the proper stroke technique. Increasing your stroke rate will substantially increase energy output and place you higher in your aerobic range. Your stroke rate will be too high when you reach the point where your breathing rate cannot remain stabilized. Coordination will be lost at this point, and you will have to slow down until your oxygen is replenished to those hard-working muscles.

Stroke rate is, therefore, dependent upon your aerobic level. As you train and as you push your aerobic limit, your aerobic level will increase—and so will your stroke rate. Our bodies are wonderful creations—as you push to excel, your total system adapts, and you become capable of achieving levels you haven't reached before. And it feels good!

The Kick. Not all coaches agree on how much benefit a strong kick has, but it does contribute to speed. Freestyle swimmers usually use six kicks for each arm stroke, although four kicks, and two kicks are used. The number of kicks per stroke is a natural cadence, and any effort to change kick frequency is probably not justified.

It is more important to know how the kick must be executed for maximum efficiency. Good kicking form requires keeping the legs reasonably straight and flexing the leg from the hips. The leg should bend slightly at the knee on the downstroke. The feet should be pointed rearward, and the heels should just break the water surface. Allowing the foot to break through the surface creates turbulence, and looks good, but reduces efficiency. Your feet should be about twelve inches apart, maybe a little less. Don't worry about too much variation here.

Kickboard practice is helpful for developing a strong effective kick. It is best to do kickboard practice each time you swim, especially when you first begin to swim. First attempts at kickboard practice may be discouraging, as you may hardly move at all. But keep at it and improvement will come.

<u>Coordination.</u> Putting all of the basic techniques together is what coordination is all about. Stroke length, stroke speed, a strong stroke pull-through, hand entry and exit, body rotation, and the kick—all must be synchronized for maximum efficiency. While doing all this, you must breathe. Without breathing deeply enough or often enough, you are not going very far or very fast. In Chapter One, we discussed the importance of oxygen; without enough of it your energy output will drop off quickly. And, you may want to go back to Chapter Two to review the importance of carbohydrates to your energy levels.

With everything else being equal, why do younger swimmers perform better than the seniors? Both may have excellent coordination. We all know that youth has its advantage. One of the reasons is in the amount of oxygen our lungs can process. Some experts claim that we lose about one percent of our oxygen capacity for each year after age twenty-five. Research with Master swimmers reveals such losses apply only to those who are sedentary. The loss is not so great for those who stay in good physical condition.

We won't bore you with any more numbers here, but it is realistic to note that the senior's reduced lung capacity will deliver less oxygen to those dependent blood cells. Reduced oxygen supply will tend to impair our coordination if we try to maintain a pace that cannot support our energy requirements.

Sports doctors often advise senior swimmers to breathe on every stroke, either on the right hand stroke or on the left, it doesn't matter. Just remember, skipping breathing for much more than one stroke will leave you breathless! Don't skip breathing while swimming the freestyle for distances of more than 100 yards, except for the last few yards in a race.

Other factors contribute to our slowing down process. The food, oxygen, and the water we have ingested must be converted (metabolized) to muscle energy. This rate slows down as we age, and that is why those youngsters are able to pass us by. But, if you are in great shape and maintain your coordination, they won't be able to do it easily. Watching the swimmer (you) glide through the water with everything working together is a joy to behold. Bring your family along to see you compete in your next swim meet. You may not win, but they will think you're great anyway. And *that's* quality time!

The Breaststroke. The freestyle stroke was described first because it is the simplest and most used stroke form. Aerobic and fitness standards developed for this book were based on this stroke. The breaststroke is the slowest of the four strokes; however, it is a competitive stroke. It is also a great stroke for easy recreational swimming. During triathlons, it is used repeatedly to be able to temporarily take a look to see if you are headed in the right direction. Accordingly, it is used in lifesaving for the same purpose.

Breaststroke Rules. Disqualification can happen very easily when swimming the breaststroke. Both hands must touch the end of the pool at the turn. As you kick off from the end of the pool, you may go under the water surface, and you are allowed one stroke and kick before surfacing. The same holds true when you go off the starting blocks—one stroke and kick before you surface. During the stroke, the shoulders must remain horizontal with the water surface. Earlier rules did not permit the head to go underwater during the stroke cycle. These rules were changed in 1986 to allow the head to go underwater as long as the head surfaces once for each stroke cycle. This change resulted in increased speed. Remember these rules, because the officials really do watch.

Body Position. Body position with the breaststroke is as important as it is in freestyle swimming. Swimming slippery or streamlining is accomplished by keeping the head down. If your head is too high, your hips and legs will drop lower in the water creating excessive drag. Swimming as streamlined as possible is essential to produce the maximum distance for each stroke.

The stroke is begun by extending the arms forward in the glide position. The palms may be extended together in the prayer position, or the index fingers may touch with the thumbs pointed down as the arms are extended. With the arms extended, the hands should just break the surface of the water. The pull begins with the palms turning outward as the hands move outward and downward. The elbows will bend slightly, and the hands will continue to extend outward as far back as the shoulders. The elbows will continue to bend as the hands return to the body at about the chest level. The elbows should remain up and should not be pulled into the ribs. The stroke ends when your hands meet at the chest just prior to returning to the glide position. The breaststroke pull is often described as forming little hearts with each hand. This technique must be faithfully followed to get decent results.

Strength. A powerful stroke is of course an asset. Breaststroke swimmers have very well-developed shoulder muscles. You can see those muscles ripple at the back of the shoulder, and those pectoral muscles are also well conditioned. One very accomplished senior lady swimmer looks frail until you watch her swim; then, those watching her are completely amazed at her speed. But, under the pale skin covering her shoulders are very well developed muscles. Development of those muscles is best accomplished while practicing the mechanics of your stroke. The more you practice, the better you will be.

Stroke Rate. Stroke rate is dependent upon your aerobic capability. As for all the other swimming strokes, you can increase your stroke rate as long as you stay within your aerobic limit and maintain your stroke technique. As you exceed your aerobic limit, your breathing rate will not stabilize; then, you must slow down to catch up on your oxygen supply. To get better, it is essential to push your limit, and during training, that limit will increase as will your stroke rate.

In any competition requiring endurance and speed, it will be necessary to remain just under your aerobic limit. You can exceed that limit for maybe as much as about fifteen seconds for that final sprint to the finish. You must train and train to know just where your aerobic limit is. Your breathing rate will "tell" you where you are. Occasionally, as you try to increase your speed, you will begin to exceed your upper limit. When that happens, drop back slightly on your stroke rate, and do it quickly. This is your fine line of efficiency; trying to swim faster will be counterproductive.

The Kick. The breaststroke kick and its timing are somewhat difficult to explain. Usually, the timing will be that which you are naturally inclined to do. First, we will describe the mechanics of the kick, and then we will get into the timing and the glide.

The kick begins with the legs fully extended and together, with the toes pointed rearward. Your legs should be close to the surface of the water. Next, your heels are brought up to your buttocks, and as your knees bend, the knees should spread apart while your feet remain close together. As your knees bend, your feet will bend downward (flexing at the ankles) in preparation for the rearward thrust. The powerful thrust is made by your legs and the inner part of your feet as your feet spread apart (about eighteen inches).

After your legs fully extend, your feet should then come together and your feet return to the original position with your toes pointed rearward. This is the classic breaststroke kick, and it is often difficult to perfect, especially if you have already established some flaws.

The glide lasts for a very short time in competition; in casual swimming it can be increased as you see fit. The glide should occur after the stroke is completed and before the next stroke begins. It may last as long as a few seconds, and will drop to almost zero for sprints.

The start of the breaststroke kick occurs as the arms are moving forward in recovery. As the arms extend forward, the legs begin to bend and the heels move toward the buttocks. The rearward push of the legs and feet begins before the arms are fully extended forward. Don't expect to get all this down quickly; it will take a lot of practice to get it right. Kickboard practice is especially beneficial, although you won't see many swimmers practice this kick—except the better swimmers.

Breathing. Throughout this book, the supply of oxygen is stressed as a primary need. How well you supply your body with its oxygen needs will have a direct bearing on how well you do. It's important to breathe as deeply as you can and exhale completely before taking that next breath. You should exhale as the pull stroke is being completed and your head begins to rise out of the water. Obviously, you will inhale with your head out of the water at the beginning of the pull stroke. So it is imperative that you completely exhale by the time your mouth rises above the water surface. Avoid short, jerky breaths.

Coordination. Until you get into the mechanics and timing, the breaststroke appears, at least outwardly, to be simple. It seems sort of like the dog paddle, only a little more complicated. Well, that just isn't the way it is. Even though the breaststroke is the slowest of the four strokes, the difference in the speed of swimmers varies widely. And, although conditioning is part of the equation, technique and coordination are of utmost importance with this stroke. With the breaststroke, timing the stroke with the kick, knowing when to use the glide, and breathing properly all need to be practiced.

It will be to your benefit to ask an expert swimmer to watch you as you swim. Basic faults can be detected fairly easily. Having someone else look at your technique and coordination and providing helpful advice will save you a lot of time. It just doesn't make a lot of sense to keep practicing mistakes over and over. When you start getting an occasional ribbon or medal at the swimming meets, you will be thankful for that advice.

The Backstroke. The backstroke is the third fastest of the four swim strokes, although its speed is very close to that of the butterfly. Two variations are used: one using the alternating arm stroke, and one where both arms stroke at the same time. Either stroke is acceptable in competition.

Backstroke Rules. The rules for this stroke are simple. The swimmer must touch the end of the pool with one hand, and may turn off his or her back to do so. But, as the swimmer pushes off, he or she must return to the backstroke position during the push-off. Competition starts with the swimmer in the water, feet up against the pool and with the hands holding the starting block rod.

Getting Slippery. The streamlined position for the backstroke can be best described with the swimmer lying in the water with the back down. The hips should be about eight inches below the water surface or maybe a little less if you are short. The distance may have to be adjusted so that, when you kick, your feet will not leave the water.

The position of your hips will be determined by the position of your head in the water. Tilting your head back will tend to raise your hips, and tucking your chin in will drop the hips down. Excessive drag will occur if your hips and legs are too low in the water. Dr. James Counsilman advised that a good drill for body position is to practice kicking with both arms extended overhead, head held back with the ears in the water and the chest lifted up close to the water.[16]

The Stroke. The backstroke pull or stroke begins with one arm extended rearward from the shoulder. The hand enters the water vertically with the palm to the outside. As you pull through, the elbow begins to bend until it is at a 90° position and your hand is at shoulder level; your elbow will be pointed down and away from the body. During the last half of the pull, your elbow will move medially or closer to the body, and your arm will extend fully as it approaches the water surface. When your arm is half way through or at shoulder level, your hand will be about 8 to 10 inches from the water surface. Your hand will then travel deeper until it extends and returns to the water surface. As the arm recovers, your palm should leave the water face up. The stroke should be continuous with no glide.

The body will roll approximately 45°, reaching the maximum amount of roll when your hand is opposite the shoulder. The roll should be automatic, but some swimmers try to do the backstroke without knowing that the roll is part of the stroke. The amount of roll will decrease as your stroke rate increases. Your head should not roll with the body. The backstroke takes practice. Older swimmers have some difficulty extending the arm directly back from the shoulder, because their bodies and joints are not as flexible as those of their youthful counterparts. So that will take some effort.

Strength and Stroke Rate. Assuming that you have mastered, to some degree, the freestyle and breaststroke, you will have developed most of the muscles needed for swimming. You

---

16. James Counsilman, *The Complete Book of Swimming,* Atheneum, New York, 1988, p. 77.

should be in good aerobic shape, and the rigors of the backstroke should not give you much difficulty. As you try the backstroke, you may find yourself huffing and puffing for the first few lengths, but that will soon go away as your body adapts.

Your stroke rate will be dependent upon your aerobic limits—that should be no surprise. Use the same techniques as discussed for the freestyle and breaststrokes, and as your technique improves, you can push your aerobic limit and gradually improve. When you begin gasping for air and you are out of your aerobic limit, your coordination will be lost. It's okay for this to happen during your practice swims, because it is necessary to push that limit to get better. The trick is not to let it happen in competition unless you are close to the finish.

Olympic swimmers also have the problem of exceeding their aerobic limit, but their condition is excellent, they are very well coached, and their recovery rate is so quick that you don't notice any difficulty they may have until that last lap. As we grow older, our oxygen recovery rate and metabolic efficiency slow down. Don't let that affect your resolve to do your best; you may achieve levels far above your original expectations.

Strength, endurance, and stroke rate will continue to improve as you practice. Most practice sessions, which are conducted to improve these qualities, should be accomplished when swimming at about 85 percent or less of your maximum breathing rate. Occasionally, go through some speed drills to determine how fast you are, while testing your improved stroke rate.

<u>The Kick.</u> Backstroke swimmers kick about six times per stroke. The kick happens so fast that it is hard to count. Usually, your kick cadence will fall in line as you practice and learn the stroke. If your kick is such that your feet come out of the water, tilt your head forward a little more. While that churning water looks impressive, the kick does little for you when your feet are in the air. To get the maximum propulsion, keep your toes extended, and follow the general rule of kicking by kicking from the hips with only a little bend at the knee.

<u>Coordination.</u> Once you have the technique of the stroke mastered, coordination will include the body roll (which is somewhat automatic), developing your stroke rate, avoiding having

your head rotate with your body roll, and keeping that kick going at about six beats a stroke. But, then, you have to breathe.

Breathing will take care of itself. You can breathe whenever you wish. You will do well if you exhale during the recovery of one arm and inhale during recovery of the other. It will take a while, and during the development of the backstroke, you will take in some water. But, as you become more proficient and get your head position properly located, the backstroke will become easier to do. Remember to breathe deeply rather than taking shallow breaths. Keep that oxygen intake as high as possible.

Butterfly. This stroke is by far the most difficult and demanding of the four strokes, and it is the second fastest. Actually, some swimmers swim faster with this stroke than with the freestyle stroke. There are a number of things that you are not allowed to do, which increases the difficulty. It will have been best for you to have saved this stroke as the last to learn, because you will have to be in great condition to do just two pool lengths. Nevertheless, don't let that stop you from accomplishing this stroke as it will put you at the head of the class.

Butterfly Rules. Both arms must go through execution of the stroke at the same time. That includes all elements of the stroke. Arm recovery must be made out of the water. Two kicks may be used: the breaststroke kick or the dolphin kick. The dolphin kick is done with the legs and feet held together. Both legs must move simultaneously without any sideways direction.

While swimming, the shoulders must be kept horizontal with the water surface; no roll or tilting to one side is permitted. Both hands must touch the pool at the same time at both the turns and at the finish of the race. That seems like a lot to remember, but it will become natural to you as you practice and progress.

Getting Slippery. Streamlining is especially important with this stroke. Head position is critical, because it must not be held too high. The combination of a poor head position and a poor kick will cause your hips to drop, creating too much drag. Improper arm techniques may also cause the hips and legs to drop. Proper streamlining will result in your hips being positioned a few inches below the water surface. It will take some practice to accomplish proper body position.

The Stroke. The stroke begins with the arms and hands at shoulder width and with the arms almost fully extended. Your hands should be in a diagonal position, palms facing outward. Begin the stroke by pulling the hands down and back with the elbows beginning to bend. During this first half of the stroke, hold your arms so your elbows are in the high position (about shoulder level). Half way through the stroke the elbows should bend to a maximum of 90°. From this point on until the stroke is completed, the elbows should continue to extend until your arm is almost straight when it leaves the water.

As your arms leave the water, they should move in a semicircular sweep over the water. Recovery over the water is mandatory. Your palms then rotate about 45° outward for the next stroke. During recovery, keep your arms and hands close to the water. The path of the stroke has an hour-glass shape, when viewed from the top of the swimmer. At the beginning of the stroke the arms sweep wide and come up close together at a point just under the shoulders. The stroke then continues rearward until the arms and hands leave the water. To practice this stroke without the kick, a flotation device, called a pull buoy, may be used to keep the legs and feet elevated. This device is held between the thighs and will work well. All new strokes seem strange at first. Each stroke requires the use of some different muscles, so it will be necessary to train these muscles and get them in shape.

The Kick. The butterfly kick used by most swimmers is called the dolphin kick. It is different from the other swim kicks, and the frequency of the kick is dependent on the stroke frequency. Two dolphin kicks are required for each stroke cycle. The kick is accompanied with legs and feet positioned together; the legs must move in unison. The feet should be pointed rearward.

The first downward thrust of the butterfly kick starts at the beginning of your stroke cycle, that is, just as your hands and arms enter the water. Your legs will be slightly bent with the downward thrust. The second cycle of the kick should begin about halfway through the arm pull, just when the hands and arms begin to straighten out and go up to the water surface. Often, the second kick is larger than the first.

The timing of the kick is best determined by someone watching you from the side of the pool. If it is not executed as described, you will want to practice it until you get it right. Getting the right timing may be somewhat difficult; however, here is another situation where a lot of practice and discipline are required.

Breathing. Timing your breathing is important, especially if you want to get a full load of that all important element, oxygen. Inhale just as you complete the end of your stroke as your hands leave the water. You will then exhale at the beginning of the arm pull. Your breathing rate, stroke cycle, and kick are all tied together, and as your stroke rate increases to the point where you begin to gasp for air, you will have just begun to exceed your aerobic limit. When this happens, make sure you are about fifteen or twenty seconds away from the finish.

Coordination. Probably the most difficult part of the butterfly is to coordinate the dolphin kick. The butterfly takes a lot of energy, and to compete will require a great amount of quality practice. But don't give up; you will be proud as you become more proficient. Start looking at that timing clock on the wall. Check your speed as you maintain your coordination. Back off a bit, when you start breathing hard and losing our coordination. Be stubborn about it, and your speed will improve—and so will your physical condition.

The Turn. Executing the butterfly turn efficiently will save you some time in competition. Even if you do not compete, you will want to do it right anyway. The rules of touching the pool with both hands as previously stated apply. Proper completion of the butterfly turn will take some work.

Try to time the touch so that it comes at the end of the recovery stroke (this is easier said than done). This will take some practice, but will result in a more efficient turn. As you touch the wall with your hands, bend your knees and bring your feet up under your body while bending your elbows slightly. Then, place one foot over the other, turn your body so your shoulders are vertical, and push off with both feet, while the bottom arm thrusts forward below the water. As you push off, you will find yourself returning to the streamlined position. When you slow down to swimming speed, kick upward and then on the downward thrust, begin your arm pull. Do not push your body up too high on the turn, and take only one deep breath as you do so.

Improving Performance

Speed, endurance, and strength are the factors that contribute to being able to swim races well. We can recognize the excellence, or the lack thereof, provided by each of these three components while observing swimmers compete. To continue to improve, for example, progressing from the beginner Category I to the next higher category, will require that you know how to train to progress to higher levels.

Getting back to Chapter One basics, we know that supplying oxygen to the appropriate muscle groups is a primary factor in getting the maximum amount of energy out of those muscles. The first burst of energy depends on the stored source of energy and lasts only a few seconds. That will get you off the starting blocks and last for a couple of strokes. Then, the anaerobic process clicks in supplying energy without oxygen for about two minutes.

The anaerobic phase is very important because it will supply energy at the beginning of all races, throughout the short races, and at the end of all races. Raising the anaerobic limit will get the swimmer off to a good start and allow the swimmer to increase power and the stroke rate for a longer time at the end of a race. Aerobic capability will carry the swimmer through the middle of the long races.

We need to know how to train to improve speed, endurance, and strength. Just swimming laps will get you to a stage or level of development from which you will not get any better.

Improving Speed. Improving speed can be accomplished in a number of ways. Various methods are used by coaches and include some form of speed drills. Speed drills will push your anaerobic and aerobic limits. Your body will adapt, and soon your times will get better. Speed drills should be done for the race lengths in which you plan to compete. No two coaches will establish a set of speed drills that are exactly identical, but the general philosophy will be the same. Speed work must be spaced correctly to get peak performance.

Speed training, also called interval training, involves swimming a specific number of pool lengths at a given speed, with a rest between drills. The four variables required in interval training are as follows:[17]

1. The number of sets.
2. The distance.
3. The average speed.
4. The rest interval between sets.

Since each individual is different, it will be necessary for the swimmer to determine the average speed to swim each interval. If you are a Category I swimmer, and your best time for 50 yards is 0:55 seconds; then, it will be necessary to determine an interval time somewhat less than race pace. For your first try at intervals it would be best to do intervals at 70 percent of your best time. So, 100 minus 70 equals 30 percent. Then, 0.30 times 0:55 seconds equals 16.5 seconds. Your interval pace would then be 0:55 plus 16.5 seconds for an average interval pace of 71.5 seconds.

The example that follows shows a simplified method for determining an interval pace in terms of the percentage of your known race pace. In the example, the race pace that was selected was 55 seconds. To use the example, (1) choose your race pace, (2) determine the percentage of the race pace that you desire, and (3) multiply by the multiplier to get the interval pace time that you want to swim.

---

17. Ernest W. Maglischo, *Swimming Faster,* Mayfield Publishing Company, 1982.

Example

Multipliers for Intervals
(Times are in seconds)

Percent Race Pace	Race Pace	Multiplier	Interval Pace
95	55	1.05	57.75
90	55	1.10	60.50
85	55	1.15	63.25
80	55	1.20	66.00
75	55	1.25	68.75

Next, it will be necessary to determine the number of intervals and the rest time between the intervals. The condition of your body will limit what you can reasonably do. Suppose you choose to do five, 50-yard intervals with a rest interval of 45 seconds at an average speed of 71.5 seconds. For your records, you could write this down as: $5 \times 50/45 = 71.5$. This is more commonly written as: $5 \times 50/1:57$ sec. $= 71.5$. The 1:57 sec. is the time for the start of the next interval (45 seconds of rest time plus the 71.5 second average speed). For simplicity, the first notation is probably the best.

These intervals should be conducted for about five weeks or more depending on how often you swim and how well your body adapts. You should do intervals for each of the distances you plan to compete in. After you have done these drills, your lactic acid level will have dropped and you will experience some reduction in discomfort. The speed time should then be decreased for another set of intervals, or you may choose to decrease the rest periods and stay the same speed. Both systems are used.

Interval training for short distances will improve your anaerobic capability; for the longer distances your aerobic limit will be improved. As long as you compete, you will need to continue to do interval work. How far you can improve your speed is up to your determination and capability. After you have reached a desired level (competitors never seem to reach that level), do a few intervals each time you are at the pool.

Please note that speed training is done in different ways and in many different sequences. Increasing your speed during drills and lowering the rest periods in between are two ways you can vary your training. The important goal is to increase your speed and push your limits; your body will adapt very nicely.

Endurance. Endurance should be achieved before speed. Usually, if the swimmer is in fair physical shape, endurance training will not be required in the shorter distances. The starting point for endurance training should be at the distance the swimmer finds difficult to attain. Practice at that distance should be conducted until the distance is easily reached. Then, speed training may be conducted.

The body will adapt to endurance training quite quickly. How long is dependent upon your physical condition, your perseverance, and enough rest periods between practices. The longer distances such as the 500 and 1000 yard events and the postal swims will require more rest between swims. How much rest you will need is a function of many factors including how much energy is spent in other activities and how quickly your body recovers. Remember what we said about nutrition in Chapter Two. Nutritional balance is needed to adequately perform, and if you are low in carbohydrates, don't expect wonders in the pool.

Strength. Genetic upper body strength is an asset for swimmers. We need to train to develop the strength we need for peak performance. But, it is necessary to emphasize that lower and middle body strength are also important. The dolphin kick, used in butterfly swimming also requires strong, well-developed abdominal and lower back muscles; and the kick used for the other strokes will require good leg conditioning. The net result is that overall body condition is vital to the good swimmer.

There are a number of ways to develop strength. Training for speed and endurance will improve strength. Race-pace training will also improve strength as well as coordination. Hand paddles will strengthen the upper body; and using kick-board exercises will work on those leg muscles. But, what about those abdominals and lower back muscles? Practicing the dolphin kick will help, but for the more sincere, some gym work may be helpful. Most gyms have machines that will help develop these areas of the body. If you are innovative or just short of cash or time to join a health club, you can get some added strength by exercising at home.

For psychological reasons, home exercise seems to require more discipline. Many who buy exercise equipment for use at home, tend to quit using the equipment not long after the purchase. Nevertheless, two exercises will be beneficial in the home. First, and you may have guessed it, are bent-knee sit-ups.

These sit-ups are done lying on the floor with knees bent. You will need to hook your feet under the edge of the bed or elsewhere to do this exercise. Do repeats, pulling yourself straight up, and then, alternately touch the opposite knee with your elbow. Clasp your hands behind your head. Start slowly with about five repetitions, rest a half minute, and then do five more. Later, you can increase the number of sit-ups without rest periods until you get to about thirty or forty. More than fifty sit-ups may be too much; use good judgment and don't exceed your capability. Those abdominals will tell you when to stop.

Lower back muscles can be strengthened by lying on the floor, stomach down, and arching your back by lifting your head and legs. Start slowly doing only a few repetitions at a time. Increase the repetitions over time until you can do ten or fifteen. This is a tough exercise to do; go easy and avoid injury. This exercise should not be done if any lower back problems exist.

Swimming Aids

Several devices are used by swimmers in training. The most common are the fins. Fins increase the thrust by the feet and thereby increase swimming speed. Use of the fins will increase leg strength and tend to increase the stroke rate. The increased stroke rate will condition the swimmer's muscles to the faster rate. Some more experienced swimmers use a shorter version of the fins rather than those long floppy ones. Fins are beneficial, although some swimmers prefer to practice without them.

The kickboard is used to improve the kick. It is grasped at the front corners. Those with poor kick technique will find that, without using flippers, their kick won't move them forward at all. Of course, fins will help, but in competition, fins are not used, so it may be best to continue to use the kickboard without fins. Eventually, your kick will improve as will your leg strength.

Hand paddles are used to develop arm strength. You will get to your aerobic limit much faster when you use them. After a while, your arm strength will improve and so will your aerobic limit.

The leg flotation device, or pull buoy, is used to increase arm or stroke strength. It is placed between the legs (thighs) and adds buoyancy so that kicking is not needed. When swimming, the swimmer's forward progress comes solely from the arms. It is an excellent device for improving stroke strength, but the swimmer must concentrate on keeping the pull buoy from coming loose. The pull buoy is used to develop strength for the freestyle and the butterfly strokes.

Most swimmers use goggles to avoid eye irritation. However, goggles will not help you to swim faster. When they leak or come unseated as you enter the water after leaving the starting blocks, you will have to reach up and pull them down from your face. That will cost you precious time. Goggles are available that will seat on the soft flesh around the eyes or on the bony structure surrounding the eyes. Some swimmers just can't get the straps tight enough to get a good seal around the eyes. Their best bet is to get the goggles that seat on the bone structure around the eyes. Often, an adjustment will have to be made to the goggles to vary the distance across the bridge of the nose. You will have to experiment until you find the right combination that fits you.

A method to avoid losing the goggles on entry from the starting blocks is to put the goggles on first, and then put on your swim cap. When diving, be sure to keep your head between your arms; this will avoid some of the problem of losing your goggles. If you choose goggles that seat on the bone, you can tighten the straps much tighter with little or no discomfort.

Competition

A wide variety of events are available to the competitive swimmer. The four basic swimming strokes are used for numerous competitive distances, individual medleys, and relays. Events are held throughout the United States and internationally. For those who have trained so diligently, the occasion for joining in the camaraderie of swimming competition is available. The United States Masters Swimming organization sponsors events on a regional basis throughout the country, and has national competition each year. Records are kept, and swimmers from the age of nineteen and up are eligible to participate.

Short-course and long-course meets are held, and records are kept for each. Short-course events are conducted in 25-yard and 25-meter long pools and long-course events are held using 50-meter pools.

A typical meet will usually cover the following format, which will include men and women swimmers. Utilizing the available lanes may involve men and women swimming the same heat. Awards are made based on times posted in age groupings of men and women separately.

Typical Two-Day Meet

1st Day	2nd Day
50 Freestyle	100 Freestyle
100 IM (Individual Medley)	100 Breaststroke
100 Butterfly	50 Butterfly
50 Breaststroke	200 Butterfly
200 Breaststroke	100 Backstroke
50 Backstroke	200 IM
200 Backstroke	1000 Freestyle
200 Freestyle	
500 Freestyle	

Notes:
All distances are in yards
Pool length is 25 yards.
Swimmers may enter no more than three events in one day.
Swimmers will be seeded according to entry times.
United States Swimming rules and regulations will be followed.

Individual medleys are conducted with the swimmer using each of the four swimming strokes at a specified distance. For example, a 200-medley requires the swimmer to swim 50 yards or two pool lengths using each stroke. A relay involves four swimmers, each swimming a specific stroke. The fastest swimmer in each stroke is chosen to make up the team. Other types of swimming events are used, which make a swimming event exciting and enjoyable.

Six
Cycling

Fitness and the Bicycle

There are well over eighty-five million bicycles in use in America today. The number of bicyclists continues to grow. The vast membership is predominated by no specific age group, because those frequenting the nation's bike paths, streets, and roads range in age from youngsters graduating from tricycles to those in their nineties. It is not unusual that cycling is so popular, because it is a great sport!

In third-world countries, the bicycle is the primary method for getting from one place to another. The bicycle is part of everyday life, because it is a necessity. Diets high in carbohydrates, along with the exercise afforded by the bicycle, provide most of the essential components to keep these people trim. Who knows what the additional benefits of modern medicine would have done to help these hard-working people?

In Europe, bicycling has been prominent for decades; it is a mode of transportation of choice for many. It is not unusual to see large groups of cyclists riding down the busiest streets on an endurance run. American's interest in bicycling began in the 1890s when our cyclers rivaled their European counterparts. But, our fascination with speed and power turned toward automobiles and airplanes, and interest in the sport declined. Many decades would pass before interest in cycling would begin an upward swing. That interest, fueled by a desire by many to improve their fitness level, seems to have revived our interest in cycling.

People who bike recreationally are beginning to recognize the advantages that the bicycle can add to their fitness. While physical fitness popularity has begun to increase in the 1980s and now into the year 2000 and beyond, interest in the sports of running, swimming, and cycling has accelerated. Bicycling provides an easy method for us to achieve anaerobic and aerobic fitness, and it is pleasant and adaptable to the older exercise enthusiast. Except for safety considerations and accidents, cycling is pretty much injury free.

Variations in the type of cycling, e.g., mountain, touring, or racing are choices for the beginner to make. A variety of different events are available. One does not have to be competitive, for cycling provides the chance to exercise just for the pure joy of doing it, whether you are out on a tour with a group or if you are on a trail ride with friends. All of which leads you into a life style of well being.

But, nothing comes without effort. Cycling for fitness is similar to running and swimming, in that to become fit it is necessary to put in your time at least three times each week. Of course, if you tend to be competitive, you will have to spend a lot more time and put in a lot of miles. It seems easier to do this on a bicycle, but it will be necessary to push your anaerobic and aerobic levels as discussed in Chapter One. It will also be necessary to maintain a proper diet as explained in Chapter Two; that is, if you want to do it right. It only makes sense that if you want to do it, why wouldn't you want to do it right? You might end up being the star in your age group, or maybe you will end up looking good. Either one or both wouldn't be too shabby.

Fitness. Speed, endurance, and strength apply to cycling as with the sports of running and swimming. By adding the bicycle, additional coordination with a machine has been added. So, in addition to developing anaerobic and aerobic levels of fitness, it will be necessary to learn to coordinate your movements with the controls of your bicycle. All of these movements, including reaching down for that bottle and drinking from it as you spin down the road, will require you to maintain your balance. And, some concentration will be involved.

Be careful with your first attempts on the bicycle. The elements of cycling will all have to be developed, even if you are in good shape physically. Cycling will place stress on muscles not yet developed. Getting to upper fitness levels will take time, and it will be necessary to adapt to the bicycle before you get into any serious training. We'll get into the rudiments of training later, but for now you will need to determine what kind of cycling interests you most.

Then, you can choose whether you want to be competitive or be a recreational cyclist. Once you determine that cycling will be your means for becoming fit, we suggest that you find a bicycle that suits your needs.

Choices. Three broad choices of bicycles exist: the mountain bicycle (with the fat tires), the touring bicycle, and the racing bicycle. There are many variations and options open to you. Any one of the three types can be used interchangeably to get you to the fitness level desired. Take your time when making a decision. You should visit some cycling shops and talk to the experts about what would fit your needs and desires. Be careful, some salespeople will sell you anything. Get them to talk, and you will find most of the people in the business are cycling enthusiasts and will talk your arm off.

Ask to try out a bicycle; most shops will be glad to lend you a bicycle for a tryout. Next best, rent a bicycle for a day. Try all three kinds until you find what suits you best. Remember, that a mountain bicycle is generally suited for rougher terrain, the touring bicycle is best used for the longer tours often taken by groups, and the racing bicycle is used for speed over short or long courses. The mountain bicycle with the fat tires will get you over all kinds of surfaces, and is less prone to punctures.

Many trails across the country are converted railroad beds and have a fine gravel surface. The mountain bicycle tire is best suited for these surfaces, but the skinny tires used on the touring bicycles can also be used. You'll just get an occasional flat tire, which, as you become accustomed to cycling, will be a rather simple matter to fix. Those skinny racing bicycle tires with tire diameters of about 7/8 of an inch and with 110 to 120 pounds per square inch of pressure are generally not suitable.

There are a variety of tire sizes, not just fat and skinny. And there are a number of wheel diameters from which to choose. The fatter tires will take more of your energy, but on pavement they will sing to you. The important first step here is to determine what kind of cycling turns you on the most; then, once that decision is made, the specific parameters of the bicycle type you choose must be made. Your size and strength will determine the size of the bicycle and the components which will make it up.

Bicycle Selection. The novice or beginner should probably buy a lower cost bicycle for the first purchase. Then, later when you know your limitations and how strong your desire for cycling is, you can buy a better bicycle more adaptable to your fitness level. For example, you may first buy a 10-speed bicycle and later decide that a 12-, 18-, or 21-speed unit will fit your needs better. Then, there is a range of sprocket sizes, both front and rear, that can be selected after most of your capabilities are known to you. Of course, where you do your cycling and the hills you have to negotiate will also be a factor in your front and rear sprocket selection (the rear sprockets are also called cogs).

Some of these later selections should not be made until you have either gotten into recreational cycling at least three times a week or into competition training. In the meantime, you will need to develop your body condition slowly and do some easy cycling. When your legs firm up and your arms and shoulders quit aching, you still need to make some decisions.

When visiting bicycle shops to select a bicycle, you will soon find that there are a lot of brands. Cost will range from a few hundred dollars to up to $5000. Custom bicycles can cost $40,000 or more. You will also learn, by talking to the experts, which companies make the better bicycles. And you will soon be thinking in terms of weight, material, fit, and size.

<u>The Frame.</u> When you first tried out various bicycles by renting or borrowing, you soon became aware that the frame was probably the first thing to consider. Frames come in different sizes, usually measured by the length of the seat tube (see Figure 7), so don't just buy a bicycle until you find the size that fits you best. You should be able to straddle a bicycle and have about one inch between the top tube and your crotch, maybe a little more for the mountain bicycle.

The seat should be adjustable so that, when sitting on it, your leg will be slightly bent with your foot level on the pedal in

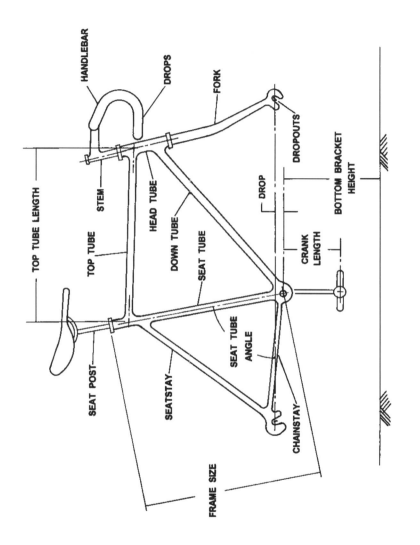

Figure 7. Bicycle Frame

its lowest position. The seat in this position should extend at least 2 ½ inches into the seat tube. The position of the seat should be adjustable (forward or reverse) so that your knee is directly above the pedal at the three o'clock position. Now, it is necessary to find a comfortable distance to the handlebars. If you have to reach too far, you will never adapt to the bicycle. On the other hand, if your position on the seat places your body too far forward, too much of your weight will be over the front axle, reducing your steering capability and rear wheel braking effectiveness. Lack of a comfortable position will play havoc with your shoulder and upper arm muscles. You can see that the seat tube angle is important in achieving the proper fit. Be stubborn about getting a good fit.

Modern technology has affected the bicycle in a big way. Frames used to be made of steel. Now the better bicycles have frames made of high strength aluminum alloys, titanium, and composites made of boron, carbon, and Kevlar fibers. The more expensive bicycles have frames that weigh as little as three pounds, maybe a little less for the smaller sizes. The serious and competitive cyclist (racer) will look for a frame that is rigid so all of his or her energy goes to the wheels. Recreational touring cycles provide some flexibility for more comfort. Serious mountain bikers also look for strength in the frame but often use bicycles with shock-absorbing suspension systems to avoid the violent shocks common to the sport.

The Saddle. Saddles are often a source of discomfort. Bicycle shorts are padded to eliminate some of the pain. Undershorts should not be worn under these cycling shorts. In addition to the upper and forward and rearward adjustment of the saddle, it can be tilted to reach an optimum position. Saddles are easily adjusted for tilt. Probably the best position of the saddle is to tilt the nose slightly downward. Too much downward tilt will tend to thrust your body forward and require your arms to support too much of your weight on the handlebars. After a couple of long rides, you will find the position that is best for you. You may opt to buy a soft seat to cover the saddle to further eliminate any soreness, but in competition these soft seats have a tendency to "grab" your bicycle shorts because they are not slick enough.

This will usually happen when you return to the seated position after pedaling standing up.

<u>Handlebars and Stems.</u> Adjusting the saddle forward or rearward will determine if you can reach the handlebars, but adjusting the handlebars up or down by raising or lowering the stem may also be necessary. You must be able to reach the brakes easily. The handlebars should be set about 1 inch below the saddle level. Most bicycles made today have the shifters located on the handlebars, so vertical movement of the handlebars will affect the use of the brakes and shifters.

Persons with a good technical knowledge and ability can make the adjustments; those who are not sure of themselves should rely on an experienced technician. All stems do not have the same design—the AheadSet design must be adjusted differently than the conventional stems. Adjustment of the AheadSet stem does not allow for any vertical adjustment, so if you buy a bicycle with this design, make sure the stem fits at the time of the purchase.

Competitive cyclists will use the drops, especially against the wind and when going downhill to reduce resistance. Consideration must be given to reaching the brakes and shifters when using the drops. You will want to place your hands on the handlebars or over the brakes and shifters when you bike in the more upright position. All of these seemingly little things will make a difference in your overall performance. Remember, it's also not out of line for recreational cyclists to be fussy about these differences that affect performance.

<u>Brakes.</u> There are several different styles of brakes in use today: the center pull, the side pull, and the cantilever brake. Some models have cable-release devices that can be used to relieve tension when the bicycle is not being used. This is a desirable function, but requires the rider to remember to restore the tension before riding, or the braking function will be diminished. Adjustment of the brakes should be made so that, with the cable in the released position, the brakes may still be applied.

Not all of the brakes sold today can be adjusted easily. It seems sometimes having three hands would help. When purchasing your bicycle, ask the salesperson how to adjust the brakes. If you decide to do the job, read the manual carefully. Make a careful trial run after adjusting the brake to be sure the job has been done properly. Don't wait until you're in a race or on a long tour to find that a shoe is dragging or the shoes do not contact evenly. Brakes are an important safety function—think about that when you are going downhill at twenty-five miles per hour or more.

<u>Gearing and Those Derailleurs.</u> A whole lot can be said about this subject. Bicycles will have either two or three sprockets in the front, called chainwheels. In the rear, as many as eight gears or cogs may be used. Chainwheels have from twenty-four to fifty-four teeth, and cogs may have from thirteen to thirty-two teeth. The combinations of chainwheels and cogs will determine the number of speeds available and the ease with which you will be able to climb the hills. A mountain bike will be geared for hill climbing, while a touring bicycle will require fewer speeds and less hill climbing capability. As an example, an 18-speed racing bicycle may have two chainwheels (in front) and eight cogs in the rear. The following example shows how such an arrangement looks.

Gearing for an 18-Speed Bicycle

Chainwheels— Number of Teeth	Cogs— Number of Teeth
53	13
39	14
	15
	16
	17
	19
	21
	23

The preceding example of gearing is suitable for a racing bicycle and requires well-conditioned legs to get up the hills. The eight cogs provide a generous selection of gear ratios so the cyclist can maintain a nearly constant number of pedal revolutions per minute over various grades. Close-coupled chainwheels, those that do not have large differences in the number of teeth, should be used for racing.

Mountain bicycles usually have three chainwheels to allow the cyclist to gear way down to make those steep hills. Sometimes even a well-conditioned and trained cyclist may have to walk a steep grade because that "old folks" low chainwheel-cog combination just won't get down low enough. Triple chainwheel sets are also often used for touring bicycles so seniors, not interested in racing, can negotiate the hills easier.

The choice of chainwheel and cog combinations should be carefully done, and it can be somewhat of a dilemma since you must choose or select combinations to meet your specific needs. If you have average strength and endurance, you may be able to choose a floor model. You may have to shop around to find what you need, but the effort will be well worth your while. When choosing a 12-, 18-, or 21-speed bicycle, you may find that you will get duplicate or near duplicate combinations, with gear ratios so close together that they are wasted or not needed.

Chainwheel-cog combinations are often expressed in terms called "gear inches." Gear inch values are determined by the following formula:

Chainwheel teeth <u>divided by</u> cog teeth <u>times</u> wheel diameter <u>equals</u> gear inches.

The following chart shows the gear inch values for that 18-speed bicycle.

Gear Inch Values for 18-Speed Bicycle
26-Inch Diameter Wheel

Cogs Number of Teeth	Chainwheel 39 Teeth	Chainwheel 53 Teeth
13	78	106
14	72	98
15	68	92
16	63	86
17	60	81
19	53	73
21	48	66
23	44	60

You will note in the chart the combinations that either duplicate or nearly duplicate each other. A 14-tooth cog combined with the 39-tooth chainwheel, and a 19-tooth cog combined with the 53-tooth chainwheel give 72 and 73 gear inches respectively. The 17-tooth cog combined with the 39-tooth chainwheel, and the 23-tooth cog combined with the 53-tooth chainwheel give identical gear inch values of 60. It is obvious that, with the increase of the number of speeds, the number of duplications or near duplications are likely to increase. Too many duplications are undesirable.

The discussion of gear inches may seem to be irrelevant. Let's look at it from a practical aspect. The term or value of gear inches is a measure of distance, which can be used to determine your bicycle speed. Consider that your bicycle is the 18-speed bike used in the previous chart, and your cadence or pedal revolutions per minute is 70. Using the 53-tooth chainwheel and the 13-tooth cog you can determine your miles per hour as follows:

Using the chart, the gear inch value equals 53 divided by 13, times 26 (wheel diameter) equals 106.
106 times 3.14 (pi) equals 333 inches per pedal revolution.
333 times 70 (pedal cadence) times 60 min., divided by 12 equals 116,550 ft./hr.
116,550 divided by 5280 (one mile) equals 22.07 miles/hr.

A lower number of gear inches will result in a lower speed, but will provide an increased ability to conquer those grades. If you don't want to go through all this numbers hassle (and most of us don't), you will have to depend on the person at the bicycle shop for advice. But if you're really a stickler for the technical aspects, crunch the numbers until you are satisfied.

Spinning the cranks at your pedaling cadence, e.g., somewhere between 50 and 90 revolutions per minute and maybe higher, will depend on your condition and strength. Your best cadence will be that with which you will feel most comfortable. Your ability to crank at the higher speeds is an asset if you can stay within your aerobic capability for long periods. The gearing on your bicycle should be chosen so you can maintain your cadence at an even rate over different grades. Of course, your cadence will drop down on those steep grades, and you will have to stand up and pedal to make it to the top of the steeper grades.

Your condition will improve as you train and get acclimated to your bicycle and the terrain you choose to go over. We'll get into the training later.

All of this discussion of gear inches and chainwheeling-cog combinations (while somewhat boring) gets us to those derailleurs. These are the complicated looking gadgets that get us from one gear ratio to another. Modern multispeed bicycles come with two to them: one in front and one in the rear. Derailleurs are cable operated, as you probably already know. The cable on the left operates the chainwheels, and the cable on the right switches the chain from one cog to another in the rear.

Derailleur shifters are mounted on the down tube, or on the newer bicycles you will find them on the handlebars (see Figure 7). Older bicycles use manual shifting without "index shifting," and the cyclist has to guess or feel his or her way to change from one gear combination to the next. Newer bicycles use index shifting, which permits precise movements of the cables to the next gear ratio desired. The good news is that most of the older bicycles can be converted to index shifting, which is a worthwhile improvement.

The price of derailleurs varies widely from those used on the less expensive bicycles to those on the more advanced models. There is a significant difference in the cost between the finest derailleurs and the second and third choices. Do not spend an arm and a leg on the more expensive brands when buying your first bicycle. As you progress in your conditioning on that first, less expensive bicycle, you will learn what you will want. Then, you can make that more expensive purchase. Use that philosophy on the other components as well.

Most derailleurs work well when adjusted properly. If you are a good technician and have an adequate set of instructions, you will be able to adjust and maintain your derailleurs. If not, rely on a reputable bicycle shop. Chains have a bad habit of coming off at the worst possible time, when the correct adjustment isn't done. Don't turn those two little screws on the rear derailleur unless you know what they are for. Contrary to most screws, these are to be adjusted, not tightened. While this bit of information is not necessary when buying your first bicycle, knowing what not to fool with will keep you out of trouble after you take the bicycle home.

As you shop for that first bicycle and before you make the more serious purchase, you will become familiar with the various brands; then, you may decide if you want to do the maintenance on your bicycle.[18] With derailleurs, you will see the names of Shimano, Campagnolo, Sachs-Huret, SunTour, and Mavic S.S.C. Most brands have various models available. These brands and others are available on the better bicycles.

Wheels. Wheels come in different diameters. The bicycles the youngsters use have the smaller diameters. Adults fifty and over will encounter two primary wheel sizes: the 26-inch (650 millimeter) and the 27-inch (700 millimeter) diameters. These are approximate comparisons, because the 700 millimeter diameter wheel actually measures about 27 ½ inches. It is best to refer to these wheel sizes in terms of millimeters, because the bicycle shop owner will not look at you as a novice. Of the two sizes, the 700 size is the most common.

You may see a wheel or tire size labeled 27 × 1¼, which is an English-American designation. The 1¼ dimension is the tire width in inches. The comparable European designation will be labeled as 700×32C, which is the metric or French designation. The number 32 is the millimeter equivalent of 1¼ inches, and the C refers to the rim width. Be careful when buying replacements, because interchangeability between English-American and French sizes is not always possible, and rim widths may not be compatible with your brakes. The ISO tire size system may help resolve the tire designation confusion, but although engineers adhere to the ISO system, this form of labeling seldom reaches the buying and using public.

If wheel sizes seem a bit complicated, you may also be surprised that the number of spokes in a wheel may vary. Wheels

---

18. "Bicycle Maintenance and Repair," *Bicycling and Mountain Bike Magazine*, Rodale Press, Emmaus, Pennsylvania, 1994.

come with 32, 36, and 40 spokes. Wheels with more spokes can be expected to carry more weight. For example, if you are 180 pounds or over and expect to buy a touring bicycle and carry additional equipment and supplies, you should consider buying wheels having more than 32 spokes. But, it gets more complicated than that because of a design called spoke lacing. You won't want to get into this technicality when you buy your first bicycle, but later, when you get in better physical condition and decide to spend some money, you will want to think about spoke lacing. Three- and four-cross lacing systems are available. For racing, the three-cross lacing is better because it is more rigid; whereas, the longer four-spoke lacing gives a softer ride, which is more suitable for touring.

To further boggle your mind, spokes come in three gauges. Most of the decisions can be left up to the specialist at the bicycle shop. They deal with the problems of bicycle selection on a daily basis. However, it doesn't hurt to have a general knowledge of the bicycle so you can ask the right questions. Once the specialist finds that you didn't just fall off the turnip truck, he or she will be more interested in helping with your bicycle selection, making you and bicycle more compatible. Besides, it's your money!

Getting Fit

Suppose you have purchased your first bicycle, and you have begun to put on some miles. After awhile, you will become adapted to your bicycle, and your legs and arms will have recovered from that initial soreness. Now, you are anxious to get a little more serious. Maybe you have seen an expert tooling down the road at what looks like maybe twenty or thirty miles per hour. You say to yourself, "Maybe I can do that. Yes I can, yes I can, I know I can!" Now you are hooked.

Getting Started. You've made a modest investment in that first bicycle, and you have decided that a leisurely bike ride once in a while isn't all that you want. You want to be good, but how good? Well, that's up to you. Your first goal should be to get in good shape, and if you are not, you will have to use that bicycle to help you tone up that body and develop those muscles. If you stick with what we are about to discuss, you will find that the body you are now concerned with will give you amazing results. Also remember—becoming competitive is not necessary. You can develop yourself by recreational cycling.

You should read Chapters One and Two, if you haven't already done so, because you are now about to embark on an anaerobic and aerobic training program much as you would if you wanted to become a runner or swimmer. Cyclists who want to be serious about becoming fit, develop into athletes even though they don't intend to become competitive. Being competitive is just another way of having fun and getting physically fit. You have to understand that getting fit is a gift you must earn!

Getting fit will require, at a minimum, that you cycle at least three times a week for periods of a half hour or more. You must start slowly and increase your distance each week. First, we recommend that you work on your endurance; that is, get your mileage up—the speed will come later. For the first three or four weeks, limit your mileage to five or ten miles per outing, unless you are in good shape. You will soon find how conditioned you are, because, as you extend yourself, your legs will "tell" you when you are going too far. If you cycle on a lot of hills, you should hold back on the mileage and progress more slowly.

If you purchase a simple mileage odometer/speedometer (one that will give you mileage and speed), it will be easy to record your results. These small devices are inexpensive and are well worth the price. If not, you will have to judge the distance and compute your speed. When you are able to go ten miles an hour for five to ten miles, you will have achieved a level where you can start to improve your speed. It is advisable to be able to spin those wheels at this pace three times a week for a couple of weeks so your body can become acclimated to this aerobic level.

Measuring Your Ability. It is difficult to set standards that apply to everyone. We all have different capabilities and have various time commitments. A mother raising children or a father who spends a lot of time on the road will have only so much time to spend on fitness. To accommodate for these variances, we have developed categories of achievement (see Figure 8),

CATEGORY I (Beginner)

WEEK	DIST. (Mi.)	TIME (Min.)	MPH	FREQ./WK
1	5	30	10	3
2	5	30	10	3
3	7	42	10	3
4	7	42	10	3
5	9	54	10	3
6	9	54	10	3

CATEGORY II (Intermediate)

WEEK	DIST. (Mi.)	TIME (Min.)	MPH	FREQ./WK.
1	9	54	10	3
2	9	45	12	3
3	10	45	12	4
4	10	50	12	4
5	10	50	12	4
6	10	46	13	4

CATEGORY III (Advanced)

WEEK	DIST, (Mi.)	TIME	MPH	FREQ./WK.
1	10	46	13	3
2	12	55	13	3
3	12	51	14	4
4	14	60	14	4
5	14	56	15	3
6	15	60	15	4
7	15	60	15	4

Figure 8. Bicycling Goals

so that, for some who have less time to spend cycling, longer periods may have to be spent to complete each category. These categories are noncompetitive levels for persons 50 years old and over, and are to be used as guidelines.

Review the categories to determine where your capabilities lie. It is better to select a category below what you think you can do, and maybe get your ego out of the way. This is especially important for men.

There is no sense in trying to go out too hard, because you may injure yourself or have to drop back or start over. That will bruise the ego. If you are in good shape because of participation in another aerobic sport, you may climb through the categories quicker. But remember, even though you may be in great shape in other sports, those important leg and arm muscles may not be ready for cycling. For most of us, no one exercise regimen is adaptable to a given set of speed and endurance parameters; therefore, you must pay strict attention to what your body is "telling" you. You can't always push yourself through the categories without adequate rest, so don't convince yourself that you can. The body will adapt beautifully, but it will break down if you are not prudent.

A final word about the three categories. It is not necessary for you to go through all three categories. Going through Category I will be just fine if that is the level that satisfies you. Choosing to go higher and maybe getting to a competitive level is great, but that is a decision for the person striving for aerobic fitness to make. It is more important to get to an aerobic condition doing what you like to do and to be able to stay there over the long term—maybe until you are ninety.

Getting Competitive

A lot of potential athletes, those who go through the categories of achievement pretty quickly, make a quick decision to go out and compete. But, the decision to compete should not be made in haste. Getting aerobically in shape is an essential fitness step, but it does not make you a competitive athlete. All of those fine individuals who race bicycles are there because of the following:

- They are in great shape for their age group;
- They are competitive;
- They train hard more than three or four times each week;
- They have the capability; and
- They love competition.

All of the preceding needs are necessary; without them your racing career may fail. Worse yet, not doing well in racing may cause you to give up an enjoyable activity, which was certainly to your benefit. Nevertheless, each of us is entitled to try. No one knows for sure just how good they can be unless they satisfy themselves by being as good as they can get. If you fit into the mold of racing regardless of your age, great, but if not, go back to one of the categories with a smile of contentment.

Any book on exercise and competition would be remiss without the reminder that diet is an essential part of fitness.[19] Any diet should include adequate amounts of water. One only needs to see or experience dehydration once to realize how important water is to your well being. Long touring runs and cycling in warm or hot weather will require plenty of water. Touring cyclists should have provisions for two water bottles.

Definitions. Getting competitive will require a knowledge of the different kinds of bicycling events that are available. In addition to a description of some of the racing terms, words peculiar to the sport are included.

Criterium. This is the most common road race in North America. In this race, everyone starts at the same time and races over courses with turns and hills testing the biker's speed, endurance, and the ability to negotiate turns at maximum speed.

---

19. Dr. Robert Haas, *Eat to Win, the Sports Nutrition Bible,* Rawson Associates, New York, NY, 1993.

Criterium distances vary and are exciting for both cyclists and spectators.

<u>Marathons.</u> These are the long races. Officially, a running marathon is 26.2 miles long, but in bicycling, a marathon may be a 24-hour time trial; events of 500 miles; or in the extreme the RAAM (Road Race Across America) that covers about 3000 miles.

<u>Points Race.</u> This is a massed-start race (everyone starting at the same time) conducted on a track. Points are assessed to lead positions each time the racers pass a certain point or number of laps during the race. It is an exciting race to watch and is somewhat dangerous for the participants.

<u>Road Races.</u> These races cover courses, usually over 100 miles long. A race may be conducted over a large loop or a multitude of loops over various types of terrain. It is often considered a great test of speed, skill, strength, and endurance. It is conducted with a massed start (everyone starts at the same time).

<u>Stage Races.</u> Stage races are point-to-point races taking place over a period of days. Typical famous stage races include the Tour de France and Tour of Spain, which is a 22-stage event covering 2447 miles. God save the older athlete who would think of trying one of these!

<u>Pannier.</u> This strange word pops up once in awhile. We usually call panniers the luggage packs that we place on our bicycle racks or carriers. Panniers are important for those who go on long tours and need to carry all sorts of things like clothing, tents, bicycle repair kits, etc.

<u>Peloton.</u> This is a strange word that you won't find in most English dictionaries. You probably won't hear it unless you talk to a European bicyclist or read about those big stage races held in France, Spain, or Italy. Anyway, if someone says, "You missed the peloton," you probably didn't see a bunch of bikers go by. Peloton is a French word meaning squad, pack, bunch, or group. So, if you happen to hear the word, remember you read about it here.

<u>Time Trials.</u> These races are usually conducted over set distances, e.g., 40 or 100 kilometers, or for a set time of one or up to twenty-four hours. Competitors start out spaced at time inter-

vals, for example, one minute or more. This race is conducted to determine the fastest time or the greatest distance if a set time is used. The race is a "lonely" test of physical capability, because you are out there all alone except for an occasional cyclist who is passing you or, if you are doing well, when you are passing a competitor.

Triathlon. This race, combining swimming, cycling, and running is probably the ultimate test of an athlete, since it is an event comprising speed, strength, and endurance in three different sports. In the Ironman, the cyclist must cover 112 miles after first swimming 2.4 miles. Shorter distances are popular, which involve swimming from one-half to one mile, biking from fifteen to twenty-five miles, and ending up with runs from three to fifteen miles. An official triathlon distance has been established as a 1.5 kilometer swim (0.94 miles), a 40 kilometer bicycle distance (24.8 miles), and a 10 kilometer run (6.2 miles). Variations in these distances are becoming increasingly popular among athletes wanting to excel in more than one sport. A surprising number of men and women over fifty are beginning to participate in the triathlon—a sure sign of an aging population that is recognizing the joy of competition.

Road Racing. Road racing comes in all of the forms described in the preceding definitions. When you finally decide to try your athletic ability in competition, it is best to get into the criterium and time trial events. Senior Olympic races are held throughout the country and are an excellent way to break into competition.

Once you feel that you are in good enough shape, enter the shorter events. You will soon find where you fit in your age group. Adapting your body to your bicycle will be of major importance. Hills will need to be conquered. Not everyone who races will agree on how to race the hills. But, you will have to anticipate when to shift to a lower gear, by doing so just before you need it. One objective is to be able to gear down so you can maintain your cadence at the speed in revolutions per minute that you would maintain on the level. As the hills get steeper, you won't be able to maintain your best cadence. How far you can go up a hill without losing some of your revolutions per minute will depend on how strong your legs are. It will take some time before you will know when to shift and when you will have to stand up and pump those pedals.

Pumping those hills will test your aerobic ability, and you will find on the long or steep hills you may pass the aerobic threshold limit and go anaerobic. Here is where conditioning plays such an important role in bicycle racing. How well you do will depend on both your anaerobic and aerobic capabilities. As you train, these capabilities will improve. One theory about getting over the top of that hill is to stand up and pump those pedals as you approach the top 10 percent of the grade. After you pass the crest of the hill, your body can return to the business of getting aerobic again. Watch the better bikers who have the experience, and try to improve yourself by learning from them. It makes sense that you shouldn't have to learn everything by yourself and make a bunch of mistakes along the way.

Doing well in competition will require a lot of miles, hills, curves, and practice. Work on endurance first, build up your leg muscles in the process, and then work on speed. It's going to take time. Meet or exceed the Category II level before you think about getting into competition. Other techniques such as drafting and making high speed turns in a group will be achieved through experience.

Criteriums. These are good races for beginners and the veteran cyclists alike. Each race involves a massed-start and immediately places the cyclist in close proximity with other bikers. These races cover various distances and terrains and provide the novice with the experience of cycling in a group and making turns at high speed—sometimes while very close to other bikers. More importantly, you will find how well you stack up with more experienced bikers.

You will get a solemn respect for safety after several of these races, and you will learn a lot about your aerobic and anaerobic limits. You can stretch these limits improving your times as you progress. One happy day when you place first, second, or third, your desire to improve will increase. There are a lot of great bikers in competition, people with excellent athletic capability; so, don't get discouraged if it takes awhile before that first trophy or medal comes your way. Those of us who started at the back of the pack had nowhere to go but up.

Time Trials. A lot of seniors' races include time trial events. These events, which start racers at intervals, are great races for developing endurance and speed. Since the racers are spaced apart, especially at the beginning, the races are quite safe. It is in these events that you will be able to test your pedaling cadence. You will learn to pace yourself because of the long distances involved. You will also exceed your aerobic threshold as you climb to the top of the hills. Your first events should be trial events; that is, do not try to go out too fast, and pace yourself below what you think you can do. You will gain very little by wiping out too early.

Time trials involve long distance; 40 or 100 kilometers are common. At the start of the race, the biker gets in position on the bicycle with his or her feet in position on the pedals. A starter will stand behind the biker, straddling the rear wheel to keep the bicycle and biker upright. These are the moments of anticipation; your heartbeat will increase as the starter begins the countdown—10, 9, 8, 7, . . . 0—and you're off. And now in this exciting moment you gather your wits and settle into your race plan. You force yourself not to go too fast, and get down to your best aerobic cadence. After you cross the finish line, you need help getting off the bicycle, you can just barely walk, your breathing is labored, and then you know you left "it" all out there on the course. What a feeling!

Experienced cyclists always hydrate themselves before a race, and some of them start drinking lots of water one or two days before the race. However, they also carry water bottles, and for the longer races without many water stations, they will carry two water bottles. You cannot drink too much water, and you won't have to worry about making a bathroom stop along the way because you will void the water by sweating. Loss of two pints of water may reduce your efficiency by as much as 15 percent. So, it is to your advantage to take in as much water as you can, because after all that training, you do not want to do poorly because of insufficient water.

Marathons. You must be in top shape to get into a marathon

and do well. Seniors will do best doing criteriums and time trials, but once in awhile along comes someone over fifty who just isn't satisfied with the shorter distance. If you are one of those ambitious athletes, go for it and train diligently.

Bicycle marathons are *very* long races. It is difficult to define the difference between a road race and a marathon because a long road race is the same. Where to make the breakdown between the two is a matter of conjecture, and to fuss about it is without merit.

The marathon is similar to the road race in that it also features a mass start. Marathons cover distances of 500 miles or more and involve courage and exceptional endurance. The marathon takes a heavy toll on the body, and races may take many days to complete. The Race Across America is a marathon of over 3000 miles. Participants exist on only a few hours of sleep each day.

The marathon, regardless of the distance, is obviously meant for those few capable and hardy athletes who have the time to train for distance and endurance. It is not a sport for those who train for a few days each week. A marathoner was asked how he enjoyed the beautiful scenery after a long, arduous race. He replied, "What scenery?"

<u>Fun Events.</u> There is a wide variety of races available to the ardent cyclist. Local clubs exist across the country. These clubs sponsor races of all sorts, whether they be time trial events at all kinds of distances or massed start events over longer courses. All of these events require anaerobic and aerobic conditioning. Your local bicycle shop can supply you with the information on local clubs so you can get started, but read this book first to get the fitness fundamentals.

Mountain Bicycle Races. The mountain bicycle (also referred to as an all-terrain bicycle) is used in races of various categories, e.g., beginner, experienced amateur, advanced amateur, and elite top-level amateurs.[20] To determine in which category

---

20. Eugene A. Sloane, *Sloane's Complete Book of All-Terrain Bicycles,* Simon & Schuster, New York, 1991.

you qualify, merely go back to the three more general categories presented earlier. You can use these levels of physical capabilities to determine where you stand with regard to competition. Be gentle with yourself, and do not enter a race for which you are not prepared. The paragraphs that follow will identify the various mountain bicycle races that prevail throughout the country. It would be wise for you to fully understand the requirements of each of these races before you compete.

The Hill Climb. These are massed-start races conducted by categories as set forth in the previous paragraph. The race length is determined by the race director and the available terrain. Since you may have to go up hill for distances exceeding ten miles or more, you will experience an "up hill" battle for oxygen along the way. Obviously, these races are not for the faint-hearted. Some races may use the time-trial start where you push yourself against the clock.

Hill climbing will require you to become capable of traversing all sorts of terrain. To do so, you will have to know when to pedal sitting down or standing up. Your position on the bicycle will depend on the grade of the climb. While it is not always possible, you should try to maintain a steady pedal cadence while going over rough terrain.

Downhills. Downhill racing usually starts in time trial fashion. The person having the best elapsed time at the bottom wins. All sorts of skills are required to finish these races. Learning to cushion yourself against the bumps will often require you to stand on the pedals and grasp the handlebars with slightly bent elbows. Control of your bicycle is vitally important, because an accident going downhill at any speed is serious. You will need to enter the easier races to gain experience in picking your path, maintaining your balance, and negotiating obstacles in your way.

Cross Country Races. The cross country race will test all of your mountain biking skills. You will need strength, endurance, and good aerobic capability. These races are from point-to-point, or they can be conducted in one big loop. Races are set up so that you will not have to travel over the same part of the course twice. The distance may vary from race to race. If possible, it is advisable to go over the course beforehand so you will have an idea of the obstacles and terrain involved. For hills, a 24-tooth chainwheel and 28-tooth rear cog are best. If you can't make it up the hills with this combination, plan to walk those most difficult grades. It is not a good idea to completely exhaust yourself pedaling up a grade when it would be wiser to walk some of the distance and still be able to finish the race with an acceptable time.

The Circuit Race. This is a closed loop race, which is ten miles per lap or less. This race requires some strategy in addition to the skills required by mountain cycling. You will need to determine the weak points of those ahead of you so you can select an opportune time to pass. For example, if you see an opponent having some difficulty getting up the hills, and climbing the hills is your strong point, select a location where you can pass. Passing an opponent will often be demoralizing to him or her, but will add some exhilaration to your ego.

Since you will be making multiple laps around the course, you may find an opponent's weakness and pass on a later lap. Aerobic capability may also play an important part of your racing scheme. Watch for racers who seem to tire in the later laps, and then choose those places to pass that are the most feasible. It may be easier to pass a tiring opponent later in the race than in the beginning when both of you are fresh.

Safety

Mountain cycling, whether done in a leisurely manner or in a race, can be dangerous because of the terrain over which the biker must travel. Road racing and recreational cycling almost always involves vehicular traffic, so it makes sense to wear a helmet; common sense would dictate that you do so. Good, approved helmets are available in local bicycle shops. Helmets are not expensive, and it is best to buy the helmet when you purchase your first bicycle. Gloves are also a good investment. Although they do not improve safety or speed, they will provide a cushion and prevent unwanted calluses from forming on your hands.

Glasses should be worn for several reasons. They help to

prevent dust and airborne matter from entering your eyes. They also prevent glare. On cloudy days, orange or yellow tinted glasses will help; clear lenses are good for rainy days, and gray lenses will help reduce glare in bright sunlight. Reducing glare is important in helping to avoid accidents, especially when you make a turn into the sun.

Toe clips and cleats keep your feet captive so you have pedal-power on the up stroke. If you have been biking without these, and change over to toe clips or cleats, be careful, because getting off your bicycle can be hazardous. You will have to remember to release your feet from the pedals or you will find yourself under the bicycle and on the ground. Not remembering to release your feet in an emergency situation can result in an unpleasant injury. Be safe and live to be an old codger so you can enjoy your grandchildren.

Seven
Triathlons

The Ultimate Athlete

People who go into triathlons are competitive. They do not choose to go into the rigors of the training required just to get into shape. Those who do so are not already in shape for one sport but probably are in condition for at least two sports. Triathletes have a strong desire to excel in everything they do in sports. They do not make good spectators unless they are helping a protege do better. In addition to a strong desire and plenty of physical capability, he or she has to have a lot of time to train. The triathlete is not a week-end athlete.

The Tough Choice

Suppose you are a good or better than average runner, and you swim several times a week; now you are looking at maybe putting it all together and starting biking. Then, let's further suppose that you think you are pretty good at all three. Great, because you will have to be in really good shape. Competing in a triathlon is very demanding and will take a lot of energy and perseverance.

Time. Time will be a major consideration, and if you work for a living, support a family, go to church regularly, and attend an occasional social function, you are going to have difficulty finding enough time to train and hold everything else together. It wouldn't hurt to be independently wealthy! Just making out a reasonable schedule for training will be difficult enough. You will have to have an understanding and supportive family or you won't be able to train in a congenial environment.

Triathlon Choices. There are triathlons and there are triathlons. It would be safe to assume that all senior athletes have heard of the "big one" called the Ironman. This yearly event consists of swimming 2.4 miles in the ocean, cycling for 112 miles, and running 26.2 miles (a marathon). Needless to say, completing this event requires tremendous endurance and ability—often under less than desirable conditions. Yet, with all that is required to train and compete in this display of physical stamina and mental conditioning in three sports, you will find seniors competing and completing!

The shorter versions, those that most of us seniors participate in, entail varying distances for swimming, cycling, and running. A recent standard version, which will be used in the Olympics, consists of swimming 1½ kilometers (0.93 miles), covering a bicycle distance of 40 kilometers (24.8 miles), and finally enduring a 10-kilometer (6.2 miles) run. While this shorter version is much less demanding than the Ironman, no athlete finishes the event with much of anything left. Standardization will prove to be valuable so that records can be kept for evaluation.

Variations of distances will continue to exist, and most of these events are fun and provide the athlete with occasions to try out his or her physical capabilities against those of their peers. Women who compete have proven to be outstanding competitors, and more of them are competing. This is an encouraging sign, because where these women go, men are sure to follow!

No triathlon is easy—long or short. But that is not to say they are not fun. To do well, you must train long and hard in three sports, and then competing will be exciting and provide a lot of personal satisfaction. The decision to go for it or not should be weighed very carefully. When you decide to train and compete, you may be fulfilling an unknown urge—let's just call it a "late-life crisis."

Competition

Chapters Three, Four, and Five covered what it takes to develop as a runner, swimmer, and cyclist. All or most of the requirements specified to do these activities will still apply to the triathlete. That is why being a triathlete takes so much time and effort. This makes sense, but how to fit the training into your schedule, and how to arrange it to include the necessary components of time and distances is a bit more complex.

The Scene. In this book, we will concentrate on the basics of training for the shorter Olympic version, rather than the Ironman. We suggest that you read and study David Scott's book, *David Scott's Triathlon Training,* if you choose to train for the Ironman and make that trip to Hawaii.

David Scott started out as a swimmer and later started running. He ended up winning four Ironman triathlons, which is an amazing feat.

But what a lot of seniors consider more amazing is that at the age of forty, he took a second-place finish. And, yet, even more exceptional are the maybe greater Ironman athletes who are over fifty, sixty—and yes, over seventy years old. Why should we say greater? Well, they have had the drawbacks of aging to overcome, and then there were those who questioned if they were in their right minds to be out there at all. Sometimes that psychological obstacle put in their mind by these naysayers was another hurdle to be overcome by these aging competitors. But no one ever said it was easy!

If you can meet the intermediate or advanced category requirements specified in previous chapters, you can probably enter into one of the shorter versions of the triathlon. For example, a triathlon including a 1/2-mile swim, a 15-mile bicycle distance, and a 5-kilometer (3.1 miles) run might be a good place to start. Use these shorter events as a trial to see where your weaknesses are. If you started out as a pretty good runner, you may find that the first two parts (swimming and biking) depleted your energy reserves, and the final five kilometers was so difficult that you had to walk some of the hills. Pacing your expenditure of energy suddenly becomes important.

Transition times, the time to switch over from swimming to cycling and from cycling to running become factors to consider. At this point, it would be well to first consider working on a training regimen that will add to your endurance and pacing that will preserve your energy reserve over the long haul. Then, of course, you will have to increase your speed, in the sports in which you are the weakest.

What to Wear. Before we get into triathlon category levels, it is necessary to discuss what you should wear for each of the triathlon segments and to say a few words about that bicycle. Most swimmers use Speedo or TYR swim suits, which create the least resistance. Goggles should be worn whether or not the swim is in a pool or in a water site outdoors. The Old Appleton triathlon in Missouri requires swimming upstream in a dammed-up creek and then back to just above the dam for the first triathlon segment. Most outdoor swims have some contamination, so it is best to keep the water out of your eyes.

Some of the better athletes continue to wear their Speedos during the bicycle race and the run and do not don running shorts. They do this to cut down on transition time. What kind of shirt you wear is up to you, but use whatever creates the least resistance, is most comfortable, and is appropriate for the temperature. Glasses, as described in Chapter Six, are also very helpful. Most cyclists do not wear gloves because of the time required to put them on and take them off.

The Bicycle. A road racing bicycle that fits you physically is mandatory, otherwise, you will be losing valuable time and spending too much energy. Some bikers use one bicycle to train with and another more expensive version to race with. A pair of racing wheels can cost $900 or more, so the most expensive equipment is often saved for racing only. Never use open pedals! Toe clips or shoes that attach to the pedals are without question the best way to go. Even with toe clips, many advise wearing shoes with very little flexibility so all or most of the energy used in flexing the foot goes to the wheels. Sound a bit fussy and weird? Well, you will be glad you took every reasonable advantage when you achieve a personal record.

The Transition. Every once in a while a race between competitors in the same age group comes down to a matter of seconds. This doesn't happen often, but in preparation for such a situation, transition times become quite important. Before entering the water, ensure that your transition area is in order. After you leave the water and as you approach your transition area, you must know exactly what to do—shoes and socks must be in place, and your shirt must be ready to go on. If you are to wear bicycle shorts over those Speedos, they should also be in position. It is best to first don your shirt; then, put on bicycle or running shorts, and finally your socks and shoes must go on. Next, any nourishment you have set aside such as water, a sports drink, or a food that is easily digested and quickly absorbed should be carried. Then, away you go.

You will come to the transition area again, so do not forget that it must be ready for you as you prepare for the running segment. Usually, there is not much to do except to change from biking shoes to running shoes, and remember, you must place your bicycle on the rack without any help. At this point, you will again have the opportunity to take nourishment. At the very least, take water.

The Transition Area. Be sure to be very strict with yourself about what items to place in the transition area and where to place them. When, planning your transition area, remember to arrange the area for both transitions. Once the area is arranged, you are the only one allowed to touch or rearrange any of the items. Prepare the area as follows:

1. Mount your bicycle in the bike rack nearest to the bicycle exit. Be sure to choose the area assigned to your age group if such areas are indicated. Set your bicycle in the appropriate starting gears.
2. Place your socks and cycling shoes in position with the socks opened up and ready to put on your feet.
3. Place your running shoes on the opposite side of your cycling shoes. If you wear socks to bike, plan on using the same socks during the run.
4. Put your running shorts (if you plan to wear them) in posi-

tion under your shirt. The idea here is to don your shirt first; then, put on your shorts.
5. Put your helmet on the handlebar of your bicycle; then, put your glasses in the helmet.
6. Place food and water under the front of your bicycle so that you can use them when you are ready to leave the transition area. Be sure the water bottle is in place on your bike.
7. Have a bicycle pump ready just in case you need it. Some prefer to use a pump that attaches to their bike.
8. Patching equipment should also be available. For triathlons other than the Ironman, it is questionable whether to include a pump and patching equipment attached to the bicycle, since a flat tire will more than likely take you out of the race. However, it may sometimes happen that a flat tire or at least a slow leak will not be discovered until you take your bicycle from your vehicle to the transition area. Then, you will be glad you took the pump along. Don't forget to take a spare tube.
9. Always take the usual bicycle tools for those early emergencies.

Training

All of the preceding discussion in this chapter should be clearly understood before you get into training. When you start training, you will want to concentrate on getting into the best possible shape to meet your ultimate goals. Training for a triathlon is more complex than for the other three individual sports. First, it is necessary to consider the amount of time needed to meet your goals, and next, a training plan will have to be established. No two individuals are the same, so developing a training schedule at appropriate levels of intensity will take some serious thought. We will get into training categories later, but first it will be necessary to discuss heart rate.

Heart Rate. Heart rate is the ultimate barometer of our capabilities. It is therefore absolutely essential for us to understand it as a measure of what we can do. Our performance and our progress will hinge upon training and competing at percentages of our maximum heart rate. Training at various percentages of our heart rate will give our body the chance to adapt to ever increasing levels of performance. Training categories that are presented later will use your heart rate as a primary monitor to achieve higher goals.

Running and Cycling. There are a number of ways to determine your maximum heart rate. First and foremost is taking a stress test on a treadmill under the supervision of a cardiologist or a trained technician. Many of us will not opt to go this route because it is a bother and is rather expensive. Nevertheless, it is well worth it. Once the maximum heart rate is determined, a percentage of that rate is used for the various training rates.

With running and cycling, a heart rate monitor can be used. These devices can be purchased for $100 or more depending on how many functions you choose. The heart rate monitor is a two-part device. One part is a strap that goes around your chest, and the other is an electronic wrist monitor that registers impulses from the chest strap. Once your heart rate has been established, the monitor can be set to beep at a predetermined heart rate. The beauty of this function is that you can train at a preselected heart rate without any guess work.

To determine your maximum heart rate using the heart rate monitor, it will be necessary to stress yourself to the limit. This method should never be commenced without taking a full physical examination and with the approval of a physician who is qualified in providing expert advice to athletes. Begin the process of determining your maximum heart rate by doing a running warmup for ten or fifteen minutes. Then choose a hill and attack it as if you were finishing a race. Do this for about five minutes (or less) to get your breathing rate elevated, and during the last thirty seconds or so go all out. During the last thirty-second period, check your heart rate three times. Your maximum reading will be your maximum heart rate. For cycling, the method can be the same, except reading the monitor will be difficult. Mount the monitor to your handlebars, and it will be easier to read. This method is a bit risky, so be sure you are in good physical condition before attempting the procedure.

Once the maximum heart rate is determined, it is possible to take percentages of the maximum rate and use these rates as training rates. Training rates are presented later in this chapter.

One other method, used by some athletes to find their **maximum** training rate is to first subtract their age from 220 and then to subtract their resting heart rate from that result. Then, take that result and multiply it by 85 percent (0.85). Take that result and add to it your resting heart rate to get your **maximum** training heart rate. Thus, using the following equation:

Training heart rate (THR) = 220 minus your age minus your resting heart rate (RHR) x the percentage of your heart rate at which you choose to train plus your resting heart rate. Training heart rate percentages will vary depending on how you want to train, e.g., hard, easy, or very easy.

Example

If you are sixty years old and you want to train at 80 percent of your maximum heart rate, and your resting heart rate is 72, then:

$THR = 220 - (60 + 72) \times 0.80 + 72 = \underline{142.4}$

Equations are tough for a lot of us, but this method is a good way to establish a training heart rate that is safe for those in good physical condition.

Swimming. The heart rate monitor can also be used to determine your maximum swimming heart rate. To do this it will be necessary to warm up in the water for fifteen to twenty minutes and then go all out for 200 yards. Read your monitor as soon as you finish. Another method and probably more preferable, is to determine your percentage of total effort based on your best time for 200 yards. You will find how to do this in Chapter Five. Here again, you will have to use an equation. It will just take a few minutes of extra effort on your part, or get help from a friend who is good at that kind of stuff.

A third method of determining a suitable standard of exertion for training purposes is the Physical Exertion method. This method helps you to determine training rates based on how hard you feel you are working during a training session. Figure 9 shows a scale from zero to ten, with ten being the maximum effort you can attain (maximum heart rate). All other levels are percentages of that level and are determined by how much effort you feel you are expending in relation to your maximum effort. This is a judgment call on your part, but if you try to assess your percentage of maximum based on your breathing rate, you will be in the ballpark. We will use this percentage exertion method in charts to follow.

Level of Performance. Aspiring triathletes usually have some experience in all three sports, but are proficient in only one or two. Very few, if any, are the best at all three sports. In fact, a good triathlete may finish third or fourth in most single events. Overall performance counts. A runner may pick up time lost in swimming or cycling. Likewise, a good swimmer may pick up enough time over competitors to make up for a less than stellar performance in cycling and running—and on and on.

The scheme is to get as good as you can be in each of the sports in the amount of training time available to you.

Triathlons are like marathons in that they are endurance events requiring not only endurance but pacing as well. For seniors, endurance requires three or more hours of continuous physical exertion with a strong will to finish. But, endurance is only the first hurdle. Races are won based on who comes in first, although second or third place are achievements of merit. And, if you don't place, setting a new personal record (PR) is also very gratifying. There's something in it for all of us!

So, once you have established that you can go the distance, it will be necessary to work on speed. Endurance comes first though—along with pacing. Triathletes who start at a fast pace will find, to their dismay, that they do so at the expense of sacrificing some of their endurance. The net result is that you must train for the distance and improve your speed as you progress. That will take time, and there are no short cuts.

Categories. Three categories of triathlete physical fitness levels are included in this book: beginner, intermediate, and competition. You may wish to stay at the beginner level of

PHYSICAL EXERTION SCALE

10- Total Exhaustion

9- Anaerobic Threshold
   Race Speed Zone

8-
   Hard Zone

7-
   Moderate Zone

6-
   Easy Zone

5-
   Warm Up
4- and
   Cool Down

3-

2-

1-

0- At Rest

Figure 9. Physical Exertion Scale

achievement and enjoy entering into local triathlons for the pure joy and camaraderie you will get. Or, you can choose to try and place—or even win—some of these events by achieving the requirements of the intermediate level. Any one of these categories will keep you in excellent physical shape.

But, a small percentage of those who desire to become triathletes will want to reach for those medals and trophies. That will take some time and effort, and for the few who want to meet their maximum capability, the challenge of excellence is an inner drive that needs to be satisfied. Often an athlete will choose to complete the beginner level and then choose to go to the next tier because of the joy and physical rewards. The choice is yours.

The three categories presented here are suggestions only. Each athlete needs to go through a program based on his or her time available. And because we are not all the same, intensity levels may have to be adjusted. Each of the three programs encompasses twelve continuous weeks, regardless of any adjustments you have to make to meet your mandatory lifestyle requirements. A twelve-week program should not be shortened unless the category you choose as a starting point is far too easy based on your ability.

Figure 10 shows a beginner's program. Note that there are three modules of four weeks each. Each module takes you through degrees of difficulty in a manner that will permit your body to adapt. Figure 10 also shows, in the upper right corner, how the easy, moderate, and hard elements of the twelve-week program are distributed. This mix is designed to distribute the level of intensities through all three sports in a manner that is easiest to sustain by your body. PE values also relate to swimming intensity and are found in Figure 9.

Figure 11 takes you through each week a day at a time. Rest, which is an all-important factor in any training program, is included in day 4 and, if necessary, day 7 can occasionally be used for additional rest. Rest will give those muscles time to heal and is essential to prevent injury. Figures 12, 13, 14, and 15 cover the intermediate and competition programs and are similar in struc-

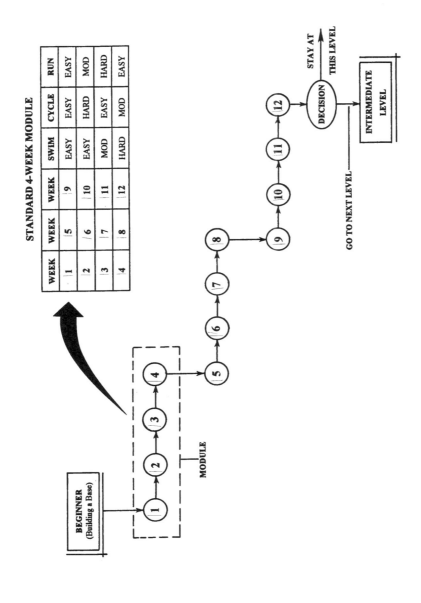

Figure 10. Beginner Level Program

BEGINNER

DAY	WEEKS 1, 5, AND 9 ACTIVITY	TIME (Min.)	HR (%) PE RATE
1	SWIM	10	PE 5
		20	PE 6
		10	PE 5
2	CYCLE	10	60
		20	70
		10	60
3	RUN	15	60
		15	70
		10	60
4	DAY OFF		
5	SWIM	10	PE 5
		20	PE 6
		10	PE 5
	CYCLE	10	60
		20	70
		10	60
6	SWIM	30	PE 6
	CYCLE	30	70
	RUN	25	60
7**	RUN	5	60
		15	70
		10	60

DAY	WEEKS 2, 6, AND 10 ACTIVITY	TIME (Min.)	HR (%) PE RATE
1	SWIM	10	PE 5
		20	PE 6
		10	PE 5
2	CYCLE *	15	80
		40	80
		15	80
3	RUN	10	70
		25	80
		10	70
4	DAY OFF		
5	SWIM	10	PE 5
		20	PE 6
		10	PE 5
	CYCLE *	15	80
		40	80
		15	80
6	SWIM	30	PE 6
	CYCLE	50	80
	RUN	35	70
7**	RUN	10	70
		25	80
		10	70

*5 minute slow, easy spin for warm up and cool down.
**Use day 7 for a day off if necessary.

Figure 11. Beginner Weekly Schedule (Sheet 1)

BEGINNER

WEEKS 3, 7, AND 11

DAY	ACTIVITY	TIME (Min.)	HR (%) PE RATE
1	SWIM *	10	PE 6
		20	PE 7
		15	PE 6
2	CYCLE	10	60
		20	70
		10	60
3	RUN	10	80
		30	80
		10	80
4	DAY OFF		
5	SWIM *	10	PE 6
		20	PE 7
		15	PE 6
	CYCLE	10	60
		20	70
		10	60
6	SWIM	35	PE 7
	CYCLE	30	70
	RUN	45	80
7 ***	RUN	10	80
		40	80
		10	80

WEEKS 4, 8, AND 12

DAY	ACTIVITY	TIME (Min.)	HR (%) PE RATE
1	SWIM *	15	PE 7
		30	PE 8
		15	PE 7
2	CYCLE **	15	70
		40	80
		15	70
3	RUN	10	60
		25	70
		10	60
4	DAY OFF		
5	SWIM *	15	PE 7
		30	PE 8
		15	PE 7
	CYCLE **	15	70
		30	80
		15	70
6	SWIM	40	PE 8
	CYCLE	50	70
	RUN	35	60
7 ***	RUN	5	60
		15	70
		10	60

*1/2 minute rest between each segment.
**5 minute slow, easy spin for warm up and cool down.
***Use day 7 for a day off if necessary.

Figure 11. Beginner Weekly Schedule (Sheet 2)

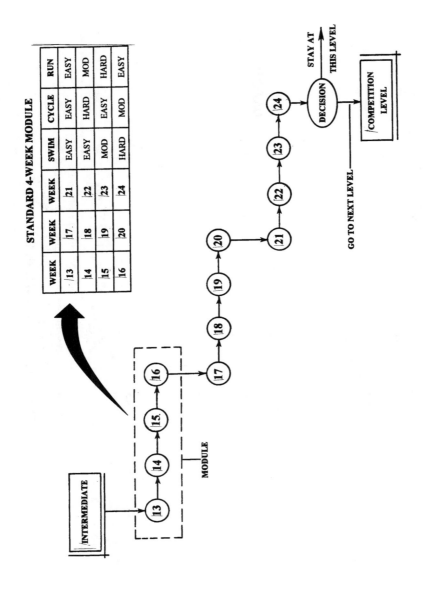

Figure 12. Intermediate Level Program

INTERMEDIATE

WEEKS 13, 17, AND 21

DAY	ACTIVITY	TIME (Min.)	HR (%) PE RATE
1	SWIM	10	PE 5
		20	PE 6
		15	PE 5
2	CYCLE	15	60
		30	70
		15	60
3	RUN	10	60
		25	70
		10	60
4	DAY OFF		
5	SWIM	10	PE 5
		20	PE 6
		15	PE 5
	CYCLE	15	60
		30	70
		15	60
6	SWIM	35	PE 6
	CYCLE	45	70
	RUN	35	60
7 ***	RUN	10	60
		25	70
		10	60

WEEKS 14, 18, AND 22

DAY	ACTIVITY	TIME (Min.)	HR (%) PE RATE
1	SWIM	10	PE 5
		20	PE 6
		15	PE 5
2	CYCLE	20	80
	*	45	80
	**	20	80
3	RUN	10	70
		30	80
		10	70
4	DAY OFF		
5	SWIM	10	PE 5
		20	PE 6
		15	PE 5
	CYCLE	20	80
	*	45	80
	**	20	80
6	SWIM	35	PE 6
	CYCLE	60	80
	RUN	40	70
7 ***	RUN	10	70
		30	80
		10	70

*1/2 minute rest between each segment.
**5 minute slow, easy spin for warm up and cool down.
***Use day 7 for a day off if necessary.

Figure 13. Intermediate Weekly Program (Sheet 1)

INTERMEDIATE

WEEKS 15, 19, AND 23

DAY	ACTIVITY	TIME (Min.)	HR (%) PE RATE
1	SWIM *	10	PE 6
		30	PE 7
		10	PE 6
2	CYCLE	15	60
		30	70
		15	60
3	RUN	10	80
		40	80
		10	80
4	DAY OFF		
5	SWIM *	10	PE 6
		30	PE 7
		10	PE 6
	CYCLE	15	60
		30	70
		15	60
6	SWIM	40	PE 7
	CYCLE	45	70
	RUN	50	80
7 ***	RUN	10	80
		40	80
		10	80

WEEKS 16, 20, AND 24

DAY	ACTIVITY	TIME (Min.)	HR (%) PE RATE
1	SWIM *	15	PE 7
		30	PE 8
		15	PE 7
2	CYCLE *	15	70
		40	80
		15	70
3	RUN	10	60
		25	70
		10	60
4	DAY OFF		
5	SWIM *	15	PE 7
		30	PE 8
		15	PE 7
	CYCLE **	15	70
		40	80
		15	70
6	SWIM	45	PE 8
	CYCLE	55	80
	RUN	35	60
7 ***	RUN	10	60
		25	70
		10	60

*1/2 minute rest between each segment.
**5 minute slow, easy spin for warm up and cool down.
***Use day 7 for a day off if necessary.

Figure 13. Intermediate Weekly Program (Sheet 2)

STANDARD 4-WEEK MODULE

WEEK	WEEK	SWIM	CYCLE	RUN
25	29	EASY	EASY	EASY
26	30	EASY	HARD	MOD
27	31	MOD	EASY	HARD
28	32	HARD	MOD	EASY

Figure 14. Competition Level Program

COMPETITION

WEEKS 25, 29, AND 33

DAY	ACTIVITY	TIME (Min.)	HR (%) PE RATE
1	SWIM	10	PE 5
		30	PE 6
		10	PE 5
2	CYCLE *	20	60
		45	70
		20	60
3	RUN	10	60
		40	70
		10	60
4	DAY OFF		
5	SWIM	10	PE 5
		30	PE 6
		10	PE 5
	CYCLE *	20	60
		45	70
		20	60
6	SWIM	40	PE 6
	CYCLE	65	70
	RUN	50	60
7 **	RUN	10	60
		40	70
		10	60

WEEKS 26, 30, AND 34

DAY	ACTIVITY	TIME (Min.)	HR (%) PE RATE
1	SWIM	10	PE 5
		30	PE 6
		10	PE 7
2	CYCLE *	25	80
		60	80
		25	80
3	RUN	10	70
		45	80
		10	70
4	DAY OFF		
5	SWIM	10	PE 5
		30	PE 6
		10	PE 5
	CYCLE *	25	80
		60	80
		25	80
6	SWIM	40	PE 6
	CYCLE	85	80
	RUN	55	70
7 **	RUN	10	70
		45	80
		10	70

*5 minute slow, easy spin for warm up and cool down.
**Use day 7 for a day off if necessary.

Figure 15. Competition Weekly Program (Sheet 1)

COMPETITION

WEEKS 27, 31, AND 35

DAY	ACTIVITY	TIME (Min.)	HR (%) PE RATE
1	SWIM *	15	PE 6
		30	PE 7
		15	PE 6
2	CYCLE **	20	60
		45	70
		20	60
3	RUN	10	80
		45	80
		10	80
4	DAY OFF		
5	SWIM *	15	PE 6
		30	PE 7
		15	PE 6
	CYCLE **	20	60
		45	70
		20	60
6	SWIM	45	PE 7
	CYCLE	65	70
	RUN	55	80
7 ***	RUN	10	80
		45	80
		10	80

WEEKS 28, 32, AND 36

DAY	ACTIVITY	TIME (Min.)	HR (%) PE RATE
1	SWIM *	20	PE 7
		40	PE 8
		20	PE 7
2	CYCLE **	20	70
		55	80
		20	70
3	RUN	10	60
		40	70
		10	60
4	DAY OFF		
5	SWIM *	20	PE 7
		40	PE 8
		20	PE 7
	CYCLE **	20	70
		55	80
		20	70
6	SWIM	60	PE 8
	CYCLE	75	80
	RUN	50	60
7 ***	RUN	10	60
		40	70
		10	60

*1/2 minute rest between each segment.
**5 minute slow, easy spin for warm up and cool down.
***Use day 7 for a day off if necessary.

Figure 15. Competition Weekly Program (Sheet 2)

ture to the beginner program, but at longer times and intensities.

A word of caution here—do not enter into any vigorous exercise without approval from your doctor. Your regular physician may refer you to a sports doctor. Those with heart disease or cardiovascular problems should get approval from a cardiologist. There are many with heart problems who are out there competing with the approval of their doctors, so don't hesitate to see your doctor for guidance.

Getting the Advantage. It's not so much that we want to beat the competitor, but that we will want to do the best we can do. You will want to win, and that will bring out your best. We could say that one is mutually dependent upon the other. In seeking to do our best, training is most important, but training alone will not get you all the way to your goals. Nutrition is important, which gets us back to Chapter Two. The right food with plenty of water will give your body the best chance to adapt to higher levels.

What happens to many or most of us is that in competition, we have a tendency to go out too fast. Yes, we discussed pacing ourselves, but in the excitement of a race our adrenaline begins to flow, and then, in spite of all of our good intentions, we're pushing ourselves too hard and burning our energy too fast and inefficiently. What happens is, somewhere down the tortuous but gratifying path we have chosen, our carbohydrates will become depleted, and our muscles will begin to rebel.

But, how do you know when you are pushing too hard? Several indications such as breathing rate and your heart rate monitor will give you a good indication. *While many athletes will go out at ninety percent of their heart rate (so called racing speed), most of them cannot sustain this level of effort for the long periods required in a triathlon.*

Many food supplements are available to help the athlete to overcome at least some of the effects of going out too hard for too long. These foods are designed to be taken and absorbed into our systems quickly. You have probably read that the food you eat takes two hours to digest. You may also have heard that a large meal doesn't get to the athlete's energy system for maybe two days. Well, food supplements such as AllSport, Gatorade, Gu, and the PowerBar do work. The supplementary drinks are often offered at water stations, and can be purchased for use at the transitions. The PowerBar is easiest to use at the transitions (easier-to-use wrappers are now available). The 2.25-ounce PowerBar provides 230 calories, which includes 45 grams of carbohydrates. Gu comes in little packages that are easy to open and can be attached to your shorts with a safety pin. Each package provides 100 calories, so when you run out of gas, one package won't take you very far. Gu should be taken with water, and gives an energy boost fairly quickly. Other quick energy foods exist, and those mentioned here are representative of what exists. You should read the nutrition label before using any of them.

These supplemental bursts of energy should not be used in lieu of meeting the long distance training requirements. Training properly will improve our ability to store larger amounts of energy, increasing the concentration of those "energy houses" (mitochondria) within the muscle cells. We didn't tell you about these in the first part of the book because they are too technical. But, these little storage centers are there, and we will draw from this storage supply as we go from point A to point B. However, it is best to prepare to use the supplements as they will help you over the hurdles when and if you need them.

Your choice of bicycles will have some bearing on your race time. There are several devices that can be used to help make your bike ride easier and more efficient. Aerobars, fastened to your handlebars, will help you to relax those shoulder and arm muscles during the ride and will conserve some energy. Water bottles are a mandatory requirement. Some athletes use a system that allows them to lean over and draw water from a tube attached to a bottle fastened to the handlebar. Low resistance wheels will also give you some advantage, but they are expensive.

Bicycle Repair. The question of whether or not to repair the bicycle during a triathlon of the Olympic distance or shorter is a choice that must be made. A flat during a race will probably take you out of contention. However, if you take a spare tube and some of those plastic tools used to remove the tire you may be able to replace a tube in about two minutes. Then, add about thirty seconds (maybe less), to pump up the tire. Patching a tube just takes too long, so leave that equipment and the wrenches, etc., back in your car.

Depending on your ability, you may be able to overcome that 2½ minute deficit. Changing a tube that quickly will take some practice. Very small pouches that can be fastened to your bicycle seat are available. Of course, a bicycle pump must be toted along too. But, both of these items can be taken along without adding much weight or wind resistance. If you are very proficient and a top-notch athlete, the option is feasible. Some triathletes are so competitive that they will do the repair, attack the remainder of the course, and live with the results.

Upper Body Strength. Upper body strength will enhance your capability in the swim and bicycle segments of the triathlon. The best option is to join a fitness center. Here, capable fitness experts can help you develop a program that will build up your arms, shoulders, and abdomen. A complicated program is not necessary, but whatever schedule is chosen, it should be accomplished three times each week. After a few weeks you may not see any appreciable increase in muscle mass, but rest assured that you are building up strength and endurance. We recommend that you stress repetitions when you exercise. You should not try to be a weight lifter; endurance is a matter of repetitions—a lot of them.

Eight
Injuries

There are two kinds of rest; that which occurs between runs, and that which is required for healing. They are both spelled the same; the first is preferable.

Causes of Injuries

The four basic causes of injuries are overuse, inadequate equipment and footwear, improper training techniques, and accidents. Running, the most difficult of the three sports, will expose you to all four causes. The principal cause of injury with cycling is the bicycle, with its adjustment to the cyclist, and the occasion for accidents. Swimming is by far the safest of the sports, and the injury most common is the rotator cuff injury. Of course, training techniques play an important part in all of the sports. Weather related problems can be found in Chapter Four.

Abrupt changes in training lead to possible injuries in all sports, most notably in running and cycling. The injuries caused by sudden changes in intensity levels often are the result of deviations from a planned training program. Common sense dictates that some form of training program should be used, so a good mix of hard, moderate, and easy days is recommended.

Some of the stronger athletes, who are not so prone to injuries, get by with informal training schedules, but for those of us who are more fragile, a training program is essential. Following the schedule will be easier than living with the long down times required for injuries to heal.

Running Injuries

Running is an impact sport, and injuries are common. Of the many Americans who run regularly, 70 percent sustain injuries, some more than once. Top runners also get injured, because they consistently strive to push their limits. Some of us are more easily injured than others. None of us is exactly the same: some have more durable knees than others, some are prone to foot problems, and on and on.

Beginning runners soon find, through injuries, where their weaknesses are, and then they should learn how to avoid further occurrences. After an injury, they should determine how to treat the injury. Obviously, it is best to carefully find aerobic limits, develop proper warm-up, cool-down, and stretching exercises, and avoid the pain and healing times in the first place. Treatment of injuries will be discussed later in this chapter.

Foot Problems. Most of the problems runners experience result from the foot striking the ground improperly.[21] Two problems that plague runners are foot pronation and foot supination. These fancy words have simple explanations. Pronation occurs when the foot rotates from the outside toward the inside as the foot strikes the ground. A supinating foot rolls to the outside. A third problem is called Morton's foot, a condition where the second toe is longer than the big toe, which may be corrected (for running) with a better shoe fit.

Foot-striking problems may cause the knee problem also referred to as "runner's knee." With runner's knee, the pronation or supination causes the knee cap to move improperly. The cartilage in the knee cap wears down, thus raw bone rubs against raw bone, causing pain with each stride. This pain will only get worse as you continue to run.

You can purchase running shoes that will compensate for foot pronation and supination, but if pain persists, a sports podiatrist can provide you with an orthotic device that will correct

---

21. Allen M. Levy, M.D. and Mark L. Fuerst, *Sports Injury Handbook,* New York, John Wiley & Sons, Inc., 1993.

the problem. It is essential to understand that once knee pain begins and doesn't go away it is time to stop running before the injury gets serious.

The foot, as with the knee, is a complicated part of the body, and it is a vital part of standing, walking, and running. It's easy to understand that the foot takes a heavy beating during a run; it is a wonder that all those skinny bones hold up to the stress as well as they do.

Stress Fractures. The metatarsal bones in the foot are subject to stress fractures, because of the tremendous impact of the foot with the ground. Stress fractures are the result of the impact of the foot with each stride and the overfatigue caused by long runs. It is true that as you accumulate a lot of miles on a regular basis the bones become stronger; however, as you increase both your distances and your speed too abruptly, stress fractures are likely to occur. A stress fracture usually cannot be seen on an x-ray, but you will know it's there because of the pain. Changing your training method can also be a culprit. As an example, a veteran runner decides to run steps, and the additional (new) stress causes stress fractures in those skinny metatarsal bones.

Stress fractures will result in pain in the upper and lower surfaces of the foot, and some swelling may appear. Any evidence of such pain means it is time to stop, whether the cause is overfatigue or some other unusual activity. The bad news is that stress fractures require rest from four to six weeks.

Plantar Fasciitis. Two types of arch pain occur among runners. One is a dull ache resulting from over-stretching or tearing the plantar fascia, the support of the foot arch. The plantar fascia is the elastic sheath or covering on the bottom of the foot that supports the arch. It runs from behind the toes to the heel bone, and it acts as a shock-absorbing pad. Overuse or poor technique on the push-off can cause this sheath to become over-stretched—or, in more severe cases, a tear can occur. This condition is called plantar fasciitis (for those of you who are fussy about names). Plantar fasciitis can be very painful. Runners who have high arches and/or are ten pounds or more overweight are prone to this injury. If you try to keep running, the pain will become intense, because as you push off on each stride you will continue to damage the shock-absorbing sheath. To eliminate this condition, it will be necessary to use an arch support in your running shoes as well as your other shoes, including in your slippers. A sports podiatrist or sports physician should be consulted for this rather painful injury.

There are other causes of arch pain, including stress fractures of any one of those many bones in the foot. One cause of arch pain may come from shoes that when laced create too much pressure on the arch. This pressure may result in a temporary loss of feelings in the toes. There is just no substitute for good-fitting shoes and a good pair of athletic socks.

Black Toenails. Black toenails are another common problem, but not a serious one. Black toenails are caused by a poorly fitted shoe. What happens is that the toenail repeatedly strikes the shoe causing bleeding. This is similar to a bruise, where bleeding occurs under the skin. As you run your foot will swell slightly, and with shoes that are a bit too tight, the nail striking the shoe becomes severe enough to cause bleeding to occur. Consequently, the nail turns black and you eventually will lose it. Don't worry, it will grow back, and you can continue running—hopefully in better fitting shoes.

Heel Spurs. You may have heard of the heel spur. This condition occurs when the plantar fascia, that sheath on the bottom of your foot, pulls too hard from where it is attached to the heel bone. A spur may then begin to grow, resulting in pain as you put pressure on it. It is also possible that such heel pain may be coming from inflamed plantar fascia. Treatment for a bone spur is a proper arch support and some rest, which will permit healing to occur. Surgery is very seldom required.

Ankle Problems. The ankle is a very durable part of the body. In spite of the large forces transmitted through it, very few serious injuries occur while running. Overstretched and torn ligaments are two causes of pain. Runners may sprain their ankles in a number of ways. Training outdoors presents hazards such as tripping over a curb or a beer can, or stepping in a hole. Typically, cross country runs subject the runner to uneven terrain where more serious injuries, such as a broken ankle, may occur. Ankle sprains may also be caused by too much foot rotation, causing over stretching of ligaments. An orthotic device and strengthening exercises will correct this problem.

Knees. We have two of these, and we need both of them. The knee is a complex joint. Sports doctors understand the complexities of the knee, but most of us don't think too much about the knee until it starts hurting. Most of the problems with the knee result from pronation or supination of the foot as previously discussed. However, if you step into a hole, stumble, or run into something, you may twist or overextend your knee. When this happens, your knee will swell up, and it will be painful when weight is put on it. The solution for a sprained knee is the RICE treatment, which will be explained later. If pain and swelling persists, see your doctor.

Calf Pulls. Calf pulls will not happen often. Calf pain will usually happen if you go out on a hard run without stretching. Each time you run, do the wall push-up or the heel drop. The wall push-up is done by placing one foot away from a wall with the other leg placed a few inches from the wall. Lean into the wall with your elbows bent and force your rear heel to touch the floor. You will feel the calf muscle stretch. Hold this position for about ten to fifteen seconds. Then, reverse the legs and repeat the stretch.

The heel drop is also a good way to stretch those tight calves. Stand with your toes on a slightly raised surface, and let your weight take your heels down below the surface. Hold this position for ten to fifteen seconds and repeat until your calves are fully stretched.

Calf cramps often come on suddenly, and the exact cause is unknown. Experience has shown, however, that cramps often happen from overuse as would be the case in a long race or if the runner has not had sufficient training for endurance events. When you are running and cramps begin to occur, do wall push-ups or the heel drop. It is possible to continue on, but the cramps are likely to recur. You will then have to stop and stretch those calf muscles again. If the pain becomes severe, gently stretch, cool down, and stop.

Cramps are not to be confused with the pain of lactic acid build-up that occurs after you have depleted your carbohydrates.

Lactic acid buildup and its related pain are severe enough. While pain from lactic acid buildup is bad enough, cramp pain is about one more turn in the vice. However, in either case, it is always advisable to stop and stretch those calves.

Sometimes runners will have to stop often during a race and either do stretches or walk for a distance and/or both. This obviously will increase your time to the finish, but that is not as embarrassing as not finishing at all. Nevertheless, if you have to stop and not finish the race do so. There will always be another race.

Back Pain. Back pain is often experienced by runners. Lower back pain is usually caused by a difference in the lengths of the legs. Minor differences, as small as 1/4 of an inch in leg length can be significant. Because of the difference in length, the body is trying to compensate by shortening the long leg with pronating and lengthening the shorter leg with supination.[22]

Back pain may also be caused by the surface on which the athlete is running. Slanted roads (paved roads are slanted for drainage) provide the condition where one leg is in effect shorter than the other. Athletes doing a lot of road training may compensate by running *against* the traffic going out and *with* the traffic coming back. It will be necessary to be *more* careful when running with the traffic.

While back pain is sometimes caused from pronation of one foot (turning inward) and supination of the other foot (turning outward) as would occur on a sloped road, pain may be caused by other conditions. Stretching, and proper warm-up and cool-down procedures may help to prevent back pain. It always helps to keep your muscles and joints warm and flexible, especially for senior athletes. If persistent pain continues, your doctor should be consulted to see if changing your running pattern may correct the problem.

Hamstrings. If you watched the Olympics on television, you are aware of the hamstring problems that occur even with

22. Allen M. Levy, M.D. and Mark L. Fuerst, *Sports Injury Handbook*, New York, John Wiley & Sons., Inc., 1993.

the most highly trained athletes. When you see athletes, mostly sprinters, go down grabbing the rear of their thigh in severe pain, you have witnessed the hamstring pull. These athletes are superbly trained for only a few events and their muscles are very strong. Their body fat percentages are low. They go all out and often exceed the limit where the muscle fibers can hold together. Hamstring pulls will occur more often when the muscles are not warmed up.

As you may have surmised, the hamstring muscles are those big muscles in the back of the thigh. A hamstring pull or tear is most often caused when the foot strikes the ground with the leg extended. Runners are susceptible to hamstring injuries when running downhill, although a hamstring pull may occur when running on a level ground, especially when sprinting or going at maximum effort. Here again, stretching is important.

Sharp pain in the rear of the thigh is the indication of a hamstring pull. This is a situation where your body is not bashful about telling you that a muscle tear has occurred. Minor pulls will heal with a few days rest. Continued running will only cause you more grief, and result in a more serious injury. With serious pulls, the thigh may swell and the area just below the pain may turn black. Serious pulls will take weeks or months to heal.

Professional athletes often are prone to various injuries because they are constantly striving to excel. And, as is apparent, hamstring pulls are often one of the injuries we see on television or at the ballpark. So often, with the spirit of competition so great, the athlete goes back out too soon, and the injury becomes severe. Seeing our role models make this mistake may send the wrong message to aspiring athletes.

Recovery from a hamstring injury must be carefully formulated. First and foremost, you must stop any serious running until the injury is healed. (The pain may be so severe that you may not have a choice.) This is difficult for those who feel guilty when they are not training or when that next race is only a few days away. The RICE method of treatment (refer to page 134 for a discussion of this treatment), is recommended for recovery. Gentle stretching is required as the healing process takes place. Stretching can start a few days after a minor pull.

Stretch by standing and placing the heel of the injured leg on a chair. The leg should be almost level. Then, lean forward and try to touch your forehead to your knee. Stretch to the point of discomfort but not so far as to cause pain. Hold the stretch for fifteen to twenty seconds. Do a few repetitions to begin with, and increase the repetitions to five to ten in a group. Increase the time of stretches and the number of groups each day as you progress.

As the hamstring heals, limited activity is suggested by trainers and sports doctors. To be on the safe side, stretch and walk first to keep the muscles flexible. Later, some light running may be beneficial, but at the slightest occurrence of pain, back off. *Always stretch before any walking or running activity.* Serious hamstring pulls take a long time to heal, so don't get in a hurry or you will re-injure that sore muscle.

Stretching during cool-down is also very important, because stretching improves flexibility or range of motion (ROM). Weight training, such as leg presses may be conducted to increase strength, but a word of caution is advisable. Increasing strength will result in decreased flexibility. Trainers will advise you that it is important to increase the number of stretches between each weight training set to improve your ROM.

To provide flexibility during weight training, proceed as follows:

1. Stretch for at least two minutes between training sets.
2. Each stretch should last at least 30 seconds during cool-down.
3. Continue weight sets with stretches in between sets every other day. Do this until pain subsides.

Quadriceps. Do you remember those hamstring muscles in the back of the thigh? Well, the ones in the front are the quadriceps. And they are big, strong, and important. You won't walk, run, or bike without them. Injuries to these muscles are not as common as those to the hamstrings. Injuries may occur when running uphill, when making a sudden jump to clear a curb or water puddle, or when pumping your bicycle uphill while standing on the pedals.

The treatment is about the same as for the hamstring pull, except for stretching. Stretching is done by standing facing the wall and pulling the foot of the injured leg up to the buttock with your hand. Place your other hand against the wall to steady yourself. Do repeats the same way as is prescribed for the hamstring pull. Always stretch gently, and stretch before any limited exercise activity as you heal. Follow the cool-down routines specified for hamstring injuries. Serious injuries, involving muscle tears, may take weeks to heal, so be good to yourself and treat yourself patiently and carefully. Running or biking too soon may result in re-injury. Use the RICE method (refer to page 134 for a discussion of this method) beginning right after the injury.

Blisters. Those blisters! Who hasn't had a blister? Blisters are caused by rubbing and friction. Shoes that are too tight often cause localized friction with the skin; the result is a blister. Shoes that are too loose or too long may cause sliding from side-to-side, or from rear-to-front. The repeated sliding will result in a blister. A proper shoe fit will eliminate most problems, but sometimes just breaking in a shoe will aggravate a tender piece of skin. Be careful when buying running shoes, and inspect the interior for any roughness.

Most runners wear socks when running. Choose socks made of materials that are less abrasive and absorb moisture. Some synthetic materials are considered more absorbent than cotton, but often cotton is softer. You may have to experiment to find what is best for you. If you have skin like leather, the choice may be easy. One-size-fits-all socks may cause blisters because of the tendency to bunch up in the shoe. If you can get an adequate fit from these socks, that is fine; otherwise, a sporting goods store may be your best bet for finding socks that will give you a good fit.

Sooner or later you will experience a blister. It is best to just leave the blister alone and let it heal. The fluid inside will dissipate, new skin will form, and the outer skin will wear away. However, the blister will often burst or break open. When this happens, trim off the loose outer skin, apply an antibiotic, and add a dressing to cover the area. Be careful not to contaminate the tender, open blister area to avoid infection. See a doctor if the area becomes infected.

Swimming Injuries

The good news is that swimming is almost an injury-free sport. In fact, it is recommended therapy for other injuries. Swimming provides some resistance training and is a nonweight-bearing exercise, which makes it beneficial for the older generations.

Swimmer's Ear. Bacteria entering the outer ear can cause infection, and an infection should be treated by a doctor. Some swimmers use ear plugs to avoid infection, these may be purchased at sporting goods stores. Some swimmers use ear drops to clear the ear canal of any moisture. If you are prone to swimmer's ear, ear drops will provide relief.

Shoulder Pain. The arm is not ideally suited for exercises where the arm is raised above the shoulder. Shoulder pain with swimmers, often referred to as a "rotator cuff" injury, may occur with all strokes except the breaststroke. Swimming long distances places a high degree of strain on the shoulder. The rotator cuff, because of the repetitive action, becomes over-stressed and shoulder pain results. More technically, the swimmer experiences deep shoulder pain caused by impingement of the supraspinatus tendon (Wow!!).

Rotator cuff injuries require several weeks of rest, followed by rehabilitation exercise. That is a tough pill to swallow for the active and competitive swimmer. Your sports doctor can recommend exercises for you to do, or send you to a therapist for rehabilitation. A free-weight program can be used to strengthen those muscles, and a qualified therapist can recommend exercises that you can do in your home using small weights. This injury needs to be treated properly or it will nag you until you do.

Knee. Occasionally, the swimmer may experience some knee discomfort. This may result from doing the turn on the breaststroke or the butterfly. Often, a slight knee injury from running or cycling may be aggravated during the turn. The solution here is to go easy on the sport in which the injury occurred and eliminate the breaststroke or butterfly stroke kick for a while.

Athlete's Foot. Athlete's foot is a common contagious infection caused by parasitic fungi. It affects the foot, usually the area between the toes, although it may be spread to other areas of the body. This infection can be controlled by drying the susceptible areas thoroughly after each swim and after each shower. The use of medicated powder will help to keep the feet dry. For those who have sweaty feet, it is also advisable to change socks often.

Cycling Injuries

A correct match or fit between the bicycle and the cyclist is very important. Every cyclist training at any level should ensure that he or she is compatible with the bicycle. Beginning cyclists often purchase their first bicycle with the idea that a good fit can be attained by raising or lowering the seat or handlebars. Because of this mistaken concept, mismatches will occur that may precipitate injuries. Refer to Chapter Six for how to select the correct bicycle to adapt to your body.

Bicycle safety is of utmost importance. Whether in a race or just spinning down the road for a "rehearsal" session, safe practices must be observed. Years ago, in the predawn darkness, a cyclist going down the road in the direction of traffic and a runner going down the same road against the traffic, met. As the result of the collision, the runner died and the cyclist was badly injured. While this is an extreme example, we know that bicycle accidents are never pretty.

Safety requires the bicyclist to go with traffic and the runner to run against traffic. Yet, even under the best conditions, it is always necessary to be extra careful, especially when visibility is poor.

Overuse Injuries. The selection of gearing in training or in a race will determine your spin rate or cadence. There is a greater chance of injury if your RPM is too low and the resistance is too high. Those big leg muscles will rebel if you continue under these circumstances for too long. It's true that some of this low RPM resistance is desirable to build up quadriceps and hamstring strength, but it is necessary to back off when those muscles tell you you're nearing your limit.

Often, a slight injury such as a hamstring pull or minor quadricep pain will occur. If continued training increases, the pain, the injury, however slight, may build up and develop into a major injury. It is prudent to back off a bit when your body gives you these signals.

Head Injuries. Head injuries to the cyclist are potentially fatal. Falls from the bicycle and collisions can result in very serious injury. Accordingly, a helmet is a prime requisite for every cyclist. The helmet used should be certified by the SNELL Memorial Foundation. Helmets may be purchased that are streamlined for less wind resistance and are good choices.

Neck Pain and Injuries. Even if your bicycle is properly fitted to your body, neck pain can occur when cycling too long with your hands on the drops. In this position, you will constantly look up to see where you are going, placing a strain on your neck. Moving your hands around by placing them on the upper part of the handlebars and using an Aerobar will help reduce neck pain.

Collisions, especially the head-on impacts, can severely affect the neck vertebrae, even when a helmet is worn. Obviously, we all try to avoid such accidents, but sometimes we may become lax or bunch up too tightly in a race and, *boom!* a potential tragedy happens. Practice will help to avoid these unfortunate spills and collisions that can result in paralysis. So adapt to conditions and know your limitations.

Training and racing conditions involving too many cyclists in a small area are not the only causes of accidents. Weather and the slippery roads also contribute to the hazards. On a dry day, a little sand on a tight curve can put you head first into an obstacle that doesn't seem to want to move.

Cycling on streets with parked cars can be the cause of a very serious accident. These innocent looking cars suddenly become a disaster when the car door opens while you are tooling down the street at ten or fifteen miles per hour. The message here is, to avoid a cycling injury, one must always be alert. It helps to know where the dangers are.

Shoulder Pain. Shoulder pain usually occurs when you first start to train and increase your limits. If your bicycle is properly fitted, this soreness will disappear after a time. Relief from prolonged pain can be reduced by changing your hand positions on the handlebar.

Hands. Hands do not normally get injured, unless you take a fall. However, most cyclists experience numbness or tingling in the hands and fingers. This condition is called nerve neuropathy. It is caused by the stress on the hands and wrist (and that nerve that passes through the wrist) resulting from hyper extension of the hands for long periods of time. Again, to eliminate this condition, it is essential to move those hands to different positions on the handlebar.

Occasionally, lift your hand from the handlebar and shake and flex it so that the numbness and tingling subside. Riding gloves will help prevent the problem and will also reduce the calluses that may tend to form on your hands.

Knee Pain and Injury. Knee pain may occur for several reasons. As we discussed before, the pain may begin because of low RPMs accompanied by too much resistance. This pain is found at the front of the knee. It is also caused by the repetitive motion associated with cycling and by increasing the endurance and intensity of training.

The vertical position of your seat to get the correct distance to your pedals must be determined. When your pedal is at its lowest level, your leg should be not quite fully extended. Your knee should be in vertical alignment with your pedal when it is at the three o'clock position. Following these general rules of thumb will help to eliminate most of your knee problems.

Excessive toeing in or out of the foot is another cause of knee problems. Under these conditions, the knee cap will not track as it should and cause too much friction in the joint. Bicycle shoes that clamp into the pedal can often be adjusted to reduce the problem. Orthotic devices may also be used to correct persistent problems.

Foot and Ankle Pain. Correct fitting shoes are more important than most beginning cyclists tend to believe. The choice of toe clips or shoes that fasten to the pedals are important. But shoes must fit properly in either instance. Shoes that are too tight will cause numbness in the toes. Pain may also occur in the upper part of the foot if the shoe is bearing down on the foot. You just don't want to get out twenty miles or so down the road and have a problem where it cannot easily be fixed.

Saddle Soreness. Every cyclist is familiar with this problem. The problem with a sore bottom is more acute with the beginner because the tender skin is chafed so easily. A softer bicycle seat may be the answer, and bicycle shorts have padding that will also help eliminate the problem. It is best not to wear undershorts under the bicycle shorts. Talcum and a lubricant will also help, especially during those long sessions. Most cyclists will find that the problem will go away after time and with the observance of these few precautions.

Exposure. The outdoor elements must be reckoned with. The sun, heat, and rain beat down on the cyclist just as intensely as with the runner. Dressing to meet environmental conditions will help to prevent sunburn and the effects of a cold atmosphere. A cold rain cannot only be mentally challenging in a race, but can result in hypothermia. If it appears that you will be cycling in a cold atmosphere or in the cold rain, wear a jacket that will keep you relatively warm and dry. You just don't want to get the shakes so badly that you have trouble steering your bicycle going downhill at thirty miles per hour or more.

Body Repair and Recovery

Sooner or later, either in a race or in training, you are going to get hurt. As you attempt to reach higher levels of achievement, the time will come when you will hurt or otherwise damage a part of that wonderful God-given body you have. The injury could be any one of the injuries we have previously described or one we have not emphasized.

Your body may have given you the "pain signal" ahead of the

actual injury, or maybe you have acquired an accumulative injury. Accumulative injuries are those that gradually grow into muscle tears, a stress fracture occurs, or you get into an overuse situation. And then, you may have stumbled over a curb or a crack in the sidewalk.

The important thing about injuries is to know what to do when you have this unwelcome experience. First, you must assess the seriousness of the injury and determine whether you need medical help or you can go ahead with the RICE treatment and get into a rest and rehabilitation program, either formal or informal. If there is any question, it is best to be on the safe side and get a medical assessment as soon as possible. Usually, medical help is available at a sporting event. In most, if not all cases, using the RICE treatment as soon as possible will be the prudent thing to do (the RICE treatment is discussed on page 134). **Do not** go into some wishful thinking mode and say, "Hey, I'm all right."

Examples of athletes who did not accept the seriousness of their injuries abound. Most of us like to see the rosy picture and try to ignore or minimize the injury in our minds. Often, macho men who suffer angina pectoris (chest or arm pain) write off the pain as indigestion and nearly die before they decide to get help. If you know an EMT, ask about how often they see such "I'm OK" situations.

To cite another example, let's talk about this man, we'll call him Carlos. During a fourteen-week training period, he stumbled, fell, and fractured his ankle about two weeks before marathon time. The ankle was swollen and black and blue. He, however, continued to train at a reduced rate and actually walked to the starting line before deciding how foolish he was to think of participating. It took eight weeks to get his poor ankle healed. What would have happened if he had attempted to run that marathon?

What we are trying to emphasize here is that you should know ahead of time what to do when you get injured. Make a common-sense decision; be professional about treating your injury, and get on with your life—the roses are still out there for the picking, and they will be in full bloom when you get there!

The RICE Treatment. This method of injury treatment is the accepted method for treatment of sports injuries, and it is easy to do. Immediate care for acute injuries during the first forty-eight to seventy-two hours requires this treatment. It will prevent further damage by reducing pain and swelling, and it will promote healing. The treatment encompasses the following:

R—Rest. Rest the injured part. Refrain from more exercise, and support the injured component with a sling, crutch, or other device.

I—Ice. Apply ice or cold packs to the injured area for 15 to 20 minutes every two or three hours while awake. Wrap a thin towel or piece of plastic around the injured area before applying the ice or pack. This procedure will reduce the swelling and pain.

C—Compression. Compress the injured area with an elastic bandage or wrap the area between applications of the ice or cold pack. Compression will help to minimize the swelling and will serve to restrict movement of the injured part. Loosen the compression during the nighttime.

E—Elevation. Elevate the injured area to permit blood to flow more easily to the injured area. Elevation will also prevent the accumulation of excess fluid in the injured part. Injured arms, hands, and wrists can be supported by slings, and the legs can be elevated to a level position and supported by a pillow.

More serious injuries will, of course, require professional medical attention. If you are in doubt, get help and head for the emergency section of the closest hospital. A good rule of thumb is, if it still hurts or limits your exercise program, see a doctor. If you become injured in a well-organized sports event, medical help will be available to determine the extent of your injury. Get help if doubt exists in your mind; don't be macho.

Appendix: Composition of Foods

This appendix contains a list of foods generally available in grocery stores and supermarkets. The list will enable you to select trade-offs from foods high in saturated fat to foods rich in carbohydrates and protein. Fat, carbohydrates, protein, cholesterol, and sodium values are listed so those on restricted diets and those who choose to maintain a nutritional balance may select the appropriate foods.

Emphasis in Chapter Two was to select foods that would provide a diet comprising 65 percent carbohydrates, 15 percent protein, and 20 percent fat. This food balance should give the required amount of vitamins and minerals necessary to sustain a healthy life style. With adequate exercise and a calorie consumption to support a desired energy level, the body will approach a satisfactory weight level.

Obviously, all foods cannot be listed. For example, dozens of cereals exist, with new cereal mixtures and combinations constantly appearing to meet market demands and pressures. The foods to be selected from this appendix are those that represent the needs of active men and women fifty years old and over. The many sugar-coated varieties of cereals marketed for children have been left out, except for Cheerios, which we didn't have the heart to leave out.

Fifteen categories of foods are listed. To find a specific food, find the page number of the category in which the food exists, and then proceed to locate the food. The categories are as follows:

Food Category

Beverages
Breads and Crackers

Breakfast Foods
Dairy Products
Fish and Seafood
Fruits and Fruit Juices
Grain Products
Fast Foods
Meats and Meat Products
Nuts, Seeds, and Legumes
Oils and Shortenings
Poultry and Poultry Products
Soups, Sauces, and Gravies
Sugars and Sweets
Vegetables

Note: Values for foods have been derived from "USDA Nutritive Value of Foods, Revised June 1991," and manufacturers' package declarations.

FOOD AND NUTRITION TABLE

	amount	grams	calories	carbos g	protein g	sat. fat g	unsat. fat g	fat g	chol mg	sodium mg
Beverages, alcoholic										
Beer, regular	12 fl oz	360	150	13	1	0	0	0	0	18
Beer, light	12 fl oz	355	95	5	1	0	0	0	0	11
Daiquiri	3.5 fl oz	100	122	5.2	0.1	0	0	0	0	11
Gin, Rum, Vodka, Whiskey										
80 proof	1-1/2 fl oz	42	95	tr	0	0	0	0	0	tr
86 proof	1-1/2 fl oz	42	105	tr	0	0	0	0	0	tr
90 proof	1-1/2 fl oz	42	110	tr	0	0	0	0	0	tr
Martini, 5 to 1	3 fl oz	84	180	0.8	0.1	0	0	0	0	1
Wines:										
Dessert	6 fl oz	177	249	14	tr	0	0	0	0	15
Table, red	8 fl oz	233	171	7	tr	0	0	0	0	11
Table, white	8 fl oz	233	183	7	tr	0	0	0	0	11
Beverages, non-alcoholic										
All Sport	8 fl oz	220	70	0	0	0	0	0	0	55
Beer, NA	12 fl oz	300	70	15	0.7	0	0	0	0	0
Club Soda	12 fl oz	355	0	0	0	0	0	0	0	78
Cola	12 fl oz	369	160	41	0	0	0	0	0	18
Cola, diet	12 fl oz	355	tr	tr	0	0	0	0	0	32
Gatorade	8 fl oz	220	50	14	0	0	0	0	0	32

FOOD AND NUTRITION TABLE

Beverages, non-alcoholic	amount	grams	calories	carbos g	protein g	sat. fat g	unsat. fat g	fat g	chol mg	sodium mg
Ginger Ale	12 fl oz	366	125	32	0	0	0	0	0	29
Lemon Lime	12 fl oz	372	155	39	0	0	0	0	0	33
Root Beer	12 fl oz	370	165	42	0	0	0	0	0	48
Coffee, brewed	8 fl oz	240	tr	tr	tr	tr	tr	tr	0	2
Coffee, instant	8 fl oz	243	tr	tr	tr	tr	tr	tr	0	tr
Fruit Drinks, noncarb, canned:										
Fruit Punch	12 fl oz	380	170	44	tr	0	0	0	0	30
Grape	12 fl oz	374	200	52	tr	0	0	0	0	22
Pineapple-Grape Fruit	12 fl oz	374	180	46	tr	tr	tr	tr	0	48
Frozen Drinks:										
Lemonade, diluted	6 fl oz	185	80	21	tr	tr	tr	tr	0	1
Limeade, diluted	6 fl oz	185	75	20	tr	tr	tr	tr	0	tr
Tea, brewed, clear*	8 fl oz	220	4	0.9	0.1	tr	tr	tr	0	1.6

*Unsweetened

FOOD AND NUTRITION TABLE

Breads and Crackers	amount	grams	calories	carbos g	protein g	sat. fat g	unsat. fat g	fat g	chol mg	sodium mg
Breads:										
Bagels, plain, 3-1/2 in dia	1 bagel	68	200	38	7	0.3	1.2	2	0	245
Biscuits, baking powder, 2 in, enr flour, home recipe	1 biscuit	28	100	13	2	1.2	3.3	5	tr	195
Buns, hamb, hot dog, enr	1 bun	43	100	18	5	0	0.1	2	0	230
Cornbread	2-1/2 sq	38	180	13.1	3.3	0.2	2.25	3.2	30	283
Cracked Wheat Bread	1 slice	25	65	12	2	0.2	0.5	1	0	106
English Muffin, enr.	1	57	120	25	4	0	0	1	0	190
French Bread, enr	1 slice	35	100	18	3	0.3	0.9	1	0	203
Vienna Bread, enr	1 slice	25	70	13	2	0.2	0.6	1	0	145
Italian Bread, enr.	1 slice	30	85	17	3	tr	0.1	tr	0	176
Oatmeal Bread, enr.	1 slice	25	65	12	2	0.2	0.9	1	0	124
Pita Bread, enr., white, 6-1/2 dia	1 pita	60	165	33	6	0.1	0.5	1	0	339
Pumpernickle, 2/3 rye flour, 1/3 enr wheat flour	1 slice	32	80	16	3	0.2	0.8	1	0	177
Raisin Bread, enr.	1 slice	25	65	13	2	0.2	0.7	1	0	92

139

FOOD AND NUTRITION TABLE

Breads and Crackers	amount	grams	calories	carbos g	protein g	sat. fat g	unsat. fat g	fat g	chol mg	sodium mg
Crackers:										
Rye Bread, 2/3 enr. wheat flour, 1/3 rye flour	1 slice	25	65	12	2	0.2	0.6	1	0	175
Whole Wheat Bread	1 slice	25	65	12	2	0.2	0.7	1	0	138
White Bread, enr.	1 slice	25	65	12	2	0.3	0.6	1	0	129
Whole Wheat Bread	1 slice	28	70	13	3	0.4	0.7	1	0	180
Bread Stuffing, moist	1 cup	203	420	40	9	5.3	19.3	26	67	1,023
Cheese, Plain, 1in square	10	10	50	6	1	0.9	1.5	3	6	112
Graham, plain, 2-1/2 in square	2	14	60	11	1	0.4	1.0	1	0	86
Melba Toast, plain	1 pc	5	20	4	1	0.1	0.2	tr	0	44
Oyster	17 pcs	15	60	11	2	0	0.5	1.5	0	200
Rye Wafers, 1-7/8 by 3-1/2 in.	2 wafers	14	10	55	1	0.3	0.7	1	0	115
Saltines, made w/lard	4	12	50	9	1	0.5	0.6	1	4	165
Triscut, reg.	7 pcs	31	140	21	3	1	2	5	0	170
Triscut, red. fat	8 pcs	32	130	24	3	0.5	1	3	0	180
Wheat Thin	4	8	35	5	1	0.5	0.9	1	0	69
Whole Wheat Wafers	2	8	35	5	1	0.5	1.0	2	0	59

FOOD AND NUTRITION TABLE

Breakfast Foods	amount	grams	calories	carbos g	protein g	sat. fat g	unsat. fat g	fat g	chol mg	sodium mg
All Bran	1/3 cup	28	70	21	4	0.1	0.4	1	0	320
Bran Flakes:										
Kelloggs	3/4 cup	28	90	22	4	0.1	0.4	1	0	264
Post	2/3 cup	28	90	22	3	0.1	0.3	tr	0	260
Cheerios	1-1/4 cup	28	110	20	4	0.3	1.3	2	0	307
Corn Flakes:										
Kelloggs	1 cup	28	100	24	2	0	0	0	0	300
Gen. Mills, Total	1-1/3 cup	30	110	26	2	0	0	0	0	200
Cream of Wheat, reg., quick, instant	1 cup	244	140	29	4	0.1	0.2	0	tr	5
Fiber One	1/2 cup	30	60	24	2	0	0	1	0	140
Granola, Nature Valley	1/3 cup	28	125	19	3	3.3	1.4	5	0	58
Grape Nuts	1/4 cup	28	100	23	tr	0.1	tr	0	0	197
Malt-O-Meal	1 cup	240	120	26	4	tr	0.1	tr	0	2
Oatmeal, reg., quick, instant	1 cup	234	145	25	6	0.4	1.8	2	0	2
Raisin Bran:										
Kelloggs	3/4 cup	28	90	21	3	0.1	0.4	1	0	147
Post	1/2 cup	28	85	21	3	0.1	0.4	1	0	175
Rice Krispies	1 cup	28	110	25	2	tr	0.1	tr	0	340

FOOD AND NUTRITION TABLE

Breakfast Foods	amount	grams	calories	carbos g	protein g	sat. fat g	unsat. fat g	fat g	chol mg	sodium mg
Shredded Wheat, bisc.	1	25	89	20	2.5	0.9	0.38	0.5	0	1
Shredded Wheat, spoon size	1 cup	49	170	41	5	0	0	0.5	0	0
Special K	1-1/3 cup	28	110	21	6	tr	tr	tr	tr	265
Sugar Frosted Flakes	3/4 cup	28	110	26	1	tr	tr	tr	tr	230
Wheaties	1 cup	28	100	23	3	0.1	0.2	tr	0	354
Pancakes:										
Bisquick, red. fat*	2.7 oz	40	150	28	3	0.5		2.5	0	460
Bisquick, reg.*	4 oz	57	240	37	4	2	6	8	0	700
Pancakes, plain, enr*, 4 in dia	1	27	62	9.2	1.9	0.5	1.3	1.9	0	115
Waffles, plain, enr, 7 in dia, home recipe, w/egg and milk added	1	75	205	28.1	7	2.7	4.4	8	59	515
Toast (see breads)										

* Does not include milk or eggs.

FOOD AND NUTRITION TABLE

Dairy Products	amount	grams	calories	carbos g	protein g	sat. fat g	unsat. fat g	fat g	chol mg	sodium mg
Butter (see fats & oils)										
Cheese, natural:										
Blue	1 oz	28	100	1	6	5.3	2.4	8	21	396
Cheddar, cut pcs	1 oz	28	115	tr	7	6.0	3.0	9	30	176
Cheddar, shredded	1 cup	113	455	1	28	23.8	11.7	37	119	701
Cottage Cheese, creamed, 4 % fat, lg. curd	1 cup	225	235	6	28	6.4	3.2	10	34	911
Cottage Cheese, creamed, 4 % fat, sml. curd	1 cup	210	215	6	26	6.0	3.0	9	31	850
Cottage Cheese, creamed, low fat (2%)	1 cup	226	205	8	31	2.8	1.3	4	19	918
Cream Cheese	1 oz	28	100	1	2	6.2	3.2	10	31	84
Feta	1 oz	28	75	1	4	4.2	1.5	6	25	316
Mozzarella, made w/whole milk	1 oz	28	80	1	6	3.7	2.1	6	22	106
Muenster	1 oz	28	105	tr	7	5.4	2.7	9	27	178
Parmeson, grated, not pressed down:	1 cup	100	455	4	42	19.1	9.4	30	79	1,861
	1 tbsp	5	25	tr	2	1.0	0.4	2	4	93
	1 oz	28	130	1	12	5.4	2.7	9	22	528

FOOD AND NUTRITION TABLE

Dairy Products	amount	grams	calories	carbos g	protein g	sat. fat g	unsat. fat g	fat g	chol mg	sodium mg
Provolone	1 oz	28	100	1	7	4.8	2.3	8	20	248
Ricotta, made w/whole milk	1 cup	246	430	7	28	20.4	9.8	32	124	207
Ricotta, made w/part skim milk	1 cup	246	340	13	28	12.1	6.3	19	76	307
Swiss	1 oz	28	105	1	8	5.0	2.4	8	26	74
Pasteurized Process Cheese:										
American	1 oz	28	105	tr	6	2.8	5.6	9	27	406
Swiss	1 oz	28	95	1	7	2.2	4.5	7	24	388
American Spread	1 oz	28	80	2	5	3.8	2.0	6	16	381
Cream, sweet:										
Half-and-Half	1 cup	242	315	10	7	17.3	9.0	28	89	98
Light, coffee	1 cup	240	470	9	6	28.8	15.1	46	159	95
Whipping, unwhipped:										
Light	1 cup	239	700	7	5	46.2	23.8	74	265	82
Heavy	1 cup	238	820	7	5	54.8	28.7	88	326	89
Cream, sour	1 cup	230	495	10	7	30	15.7	48	102	123
Cream, sour	1 tbsp	12	25	1	tr	1.6	0.8	3	5	6
Ice Cream (see desserts)										

FOOD AND NUTRITION TABLE

Dairy Products	amount	grams	calories	carbos g	protein g	sat. fat g	unsat. fat g	fat g	chol mg	sodium mg
Milk:										
Whole (3.3% butter fat)*	1 cup	244	150	11	8	5.1	2.7	8	33	120
Lowfat (2% fat)*	1 cup	244	120	12	8	2.9	1.6	5	18	122
Lowfat (1% fat)*	1 cup	244	100	12	8	1.6	0.8	3	10	123
Nonfat (skim)*	1 cup	245	85	12	8	0.3	0.1	tr	4	126
Buttermilk	1 cup	245	100	12	8	1.3	0.7	2	9	257
Canned Milk:										
Condensed, sweetened	1 cup	306	980	166	24	16.8	8.4	27	104	389
Evaporated:										
Whole Milk	1 cup	252	340	25	17	11.6	6.5	19	74	267
Skim Milk	1 cup	255	200	29	19	0.3	0.2	1	9	293
Chocolate, reg.	1 cup	250	210	26	8	5.3	2.8	8	31	149
Chocolate, lowfat (2%)	1 cup	250	180	26	8	3.1	1.7	5	17	151
Chocolate, lowfat (1%)	1 cup	250	160	26	8	1.5	0.9	3	7	152
Eggnog (commercial)	1 cup	254	340	34	10	11.3	6.6	19	149	138

*No milk solids added.

FOOD AND NUTRITION TABLE

Dairy Products	amount	grams	calories	carbos g	protein g	sat. fat g	unsat. fat g	fat g	chol mg	sodium mg
Malted Milk:										
Chocolate, 8 oz whole milk, 3/4 oz powder	1 serving	265	235	29	9	5.5	3.1	9	34	168
Natural, 8 oz whole milk, 3/4 oz powder	1 serving	265	235	27	11	6.0	3.5	10	37	215
Milk Shake, thick:										
Chocolate	10 oz cont.	283	335	60	9	4.8	2.5	8	30	314
Vanilla	10 oz cont.	283	315	50	11	5.3	2.8	9	33	270
Sherbet (2% fat)	1 cup	193	270	59	2	2.4	1.2	4	14	88
Yogurt, w/added milk solids, lowfat milk:										
Fruit Flavored	8 oz cont.	227	230	43	10	1.6	0.8	2	10	133
Plain	8 oz cont.	227	145	16	12	2.3	1.1	4	14	159
Yogurt, wo/added milk solids, whole milk	8 oz cont.	227	140	11	8	4.8	2.2	7	29	105

FOOD AND NUTRITION TABLE

Fish and Seafood	amount	grams	calories	carbos g	protein g	sat. fat g	unsat. fat g	fat g	chol mg	sodium mg
Clams, raw	3 oz	85	65	2	11	0.3	0.6	1	43	102
Crabmeat, canned	1 cup	135	135	1	23	0.5	2.2	3	135	1,350
Fish Sticks, frozen	1 stick	28	70	4	6	0.8	2.2	3	26	53
Founder or Sole, w/butter and lemon juice, baked	3 oz	85	120	tr	16	3.2	2.0	6	68	145
Haddock, breaded, fried	3 oz	85	175	7	17	2.4	6.3	9	75	123
Halibut, broiled, w/butter and lemon juice	3 oz	85	140	tr	20	3.3	2.3	6	62	103
Herring, pickled	3 oz	85	190	0	17	4.3	7.7	13	85	850
Ocean Perch, breaded, fried	1 fillet	85	185	7	16	2.6	7.4	11	66	138
Oysters, raw	1 cup	240	160	8	20	1.4	1.9	4	120	175
Oysters, breaded, fried	1 oyster	45	90	5	5	1.4	3.5	5	35	70
Salmon, baked, red	3 oz	85	140	0	21	1.2	3.8	5	60	55
Salmon, smoked	3 oz	85	150	0	18	2.6	4.6	8	51	1,700
Scallops, breaded, frozen, reheated	6 scallops	90	195	10	15	2.5	6.6	10	70	298
Shrimp, french fried	7 med	85	200	11	16	2.5	6.7	10	168	384

FOOD AND NUTRITION TABLE

Fish and Seafood	amount	grams	calories	carbos g	protein g	sat. fat g	unsat. fat g	fat g	chol mg	sodium mg
Trout, broiled, w/ butter and lemon juice	3 oz	85	175	tr	21	4.1	4.5	9	71	122
Tuna, canned, oil pack, chunk, light	3 oz	85	165	0	24	1.4	5.0	7	55	303
Tuna, water pack, solid white	3 oz	85	135	0	30	0.3	0.5	1	48	468
Tuna Salad*	1 cup	205	375	19	33	3.3	14.1	19	80	877

*With drained chunk light tuna, celery, onion, pickle, relish, and mayonnaise-type salad dressing.

FOOD AND NUTRITION TABLE

Fruits and Juices	amount	grams	calories	carbos g	protein g	sat. fat g	unsat. fat g	fat g	chol mg	sodium mg
Apples, unpealed, w/o cores, 2-3/4 in dia	1	138	80	21	tr	0.1	0.1	tr	0	tr
Apples, pealed and sliced	1 cup	110	65	16	tr	0.1	0.2	tr	0	tr
Apple Juice	1 cup	248	115	29	tr	tr	0.2	0	0	7
Apple Sauce, canned:										
Sweetened	1 cup	255	195	51	tr	0.1	0.1	8	tr	8
Unsweetened*	1 cup	244	105	28	tr	tr	tr	tr	0	5
Apricots, raw, w/o pits, 12/lb w/pits	1 cup	106	50	12	1	tr	0.3	tr	0	1
Apricots, canned:										
Heavy syrup pack	1 cup	258	215	55	1	tr	0.1	tr	0	10
Juice pack	1 cup	248	120	31	2	tr	tr	tr	0	10
Apricots, dried, uncooked, 28 large or 37 med.	1 cup	130	310	80	5	tr	0.4	1	0	13
Avacados, raw, whole, w/o skin and seed:										
Calif., 2/lb w/skin and seed	1 cup	173	305	12	4	4.5	22.9	30	0	21
Fla., 1/lb w/skin and seed	1 cup	304	340	27	5	5.3	19.3	27	0	15

149

FOOD AND NUTRITION TABLE

Fruits and Juices	amount	grams	calories	carbos g	protein g	sat. fat g	unsat. fat g	fat g	chol mg	sodium mg
Bananas, raw, wo/peel:										
Whole, 2-1/2/ lb w/peel	1	114	105	27	1	0.2	0.1	1	0	1
Sliced	1 cup	150	140	35	2	0.3	0.2	1	0	2
Blackberries, raw	1 cup	144	75	18	1	0.2	0.2	1	0	tr
Blueberries:										
Raw	1 cup	145	80	20	1	tr	0.4	1	0	9
Frozen, sweetened	10 oz cont	284	230	62	1	tr	0.3	tr	0	3
Frozen, sweetened	1 cup	230	185	50	1	tr	0.1	tr	0	2
Cherries, sweet, raw, pitted w/o stems	10	68	50	11	1	0.1	0.4	1	0	tr
Cranberry Juice, cocktail, bottled, sweetened	1 cup	253	145	38	tr	tr	0.1	tr	0	10
Cranberry Sauce, sweetened, canned, strained	1 cup	277	420	108	1	tr	0.3	tr	0	80
Dates, whole, w/o pits	10	83	230	61	2	0.1	0.1	tr	0	2
Figs, dried	10	187	475	122	6	0.4	1.5	2	0	21

FOOD AND NUTRITION TABLE

Fruits and Juices	amount	grams	calories	carbos g	protein g	sat. fat g	unsat. fat g	fat g	chol mg	sodium mg
Fruit Cocktail, canned, fruit and liquid:										
Heavy syrup pack	1 cup	255	185	48	1	tr	0.1	tr	0	15
Juice Pack	1 cup	248	115	29	1	tr	tr	tr	0	10
Grapefruit, raw, w/o peel, membrane and seeds, 3-3/4 in dia	1/2	120	40	10	1	tr	tr	tr	0	tr
Grapefruit, canned, sections, w/syrup	1 cup	254	150	39	1	tr	0.1	tr	0	5
Grapefruit Juice:										
Raw	1 cup	247	95	23	1	tr	0.1	tr	0	2
Canned:										
Unsweetened	1 cup	247	95	22	1	tr	0.1	tr	0	2
Sweetened	1 cup	250	115	28	1	tr	0.1	tr	0	5
Frozen Concentrate, unsweetened, diluted	1 cup	247	100	24	1	tr	0.1	tr	0	2
Grapes, European type, raw:										
Thompson, seedless	10	50	35	9	tr	0.1	0.1	tr	0	1

FOOD AND NUTRITION TABLE

Fruits and Juices	amount	grams	calories	carbos g	protein g	sat. fat g	unsat. fat g	fat g	chol mg	sodium mg
Grapes, European type, raw (Cont'd)										
Tokay & Emperor, seeded types	10	57	40	10	tr	0.1	0.1	tr	0	1
Grape Juice:										
Canned or Bottled	1 cup	253	155	38	1	0.1	0.1	tr	0	8
Frozen Concentrate, sweetened, diluted	1 cup	250	125	32	tr	0.1	0.1	tr	0	5
Kiwifruit, raw, w/o skin	1	76	45	11	1	tr	0.2	tr	0	4
Lemon Juice:										
Raw	1 cup	244	60	21	1	tr	tr	tr	0	2
Canned or Bottled	1 cup	244	50	16	1	0	0.2	1	0	51
Lime Juice:										
Raw	1 cup	246	65	22	1	tr	0.1	tr	0	2
Canned, unsweetened	1 cup	246	50	16	1	0.1	0.3	1	0	39

FOOD AND NUTRITION TABLE

Fruits and Juices	amount	grams	calories	carbos g	protein g	sat. fat g	unsat. fat g	fat g	chol mg	sodium mg
Melons, raw, w/o rind and cavity contents:										
Cantaloup, orange flesh, 5 in dia, 2-1/3 lb whole	1/2 melon	267	95	22	2	0.1	0.4	1	0	24
Honeydew, 6-1/2 in dia, 5-1/4 lb whole	1/10 melon	129	45	12	1	tr	0.1	tr	0	13
Nectarines, raw, w/o pits, 3/lb w/pits	1	136	65	16	1	0.1	0.5	1	0	tr
Oranges, raw, sections, w/o membrane	1 cup	180	85	21	2	tr	tr	tr	0	tr
Orange Juice:										
Raw, all varieties	1 cup	248	110	26	2	0.1	0.2	tr	0	2
Canned, unsweetened	1 cup	249	105	25	1	tr	0.2	tr	0	5
Chilled	1 cup	249	110	25	2	0.1	0.3	1	0	2
Frozen Concentrate, diluted	1 cup	249	110	27	2	tr	tr	tr	0	2
Orange & Grapefruit Juice, canned	1 cup	247	105	25	1	tr	tr	tr	0	7

FOOD AND NUTRITION TABLE

Fruits and Juices	amount	grams	calories	carbos g	protein g	sat. fat g	unsat. fat g	fat g	chol mg	sodium mg
Peaches, raw:										
Whole, 2-1/2 in dia, peeled and pitted, 4/lb w/peels and pits	1	87	35	10	1	tr	tr	tr	0	tr
Sliced	1 cup	170	75	19	1	tr	0.2	tr	0	tr
Peaches, canned, fruit and liquid:										
Heavy Syrup Pack	1 cup	256	190	51	1	tr	0.2	tr	0	15
Juice Pack	1 cup	248	110	29	2	tr	tr	tr	0	10
Pears, raw, cored:										
Barlett, 2-1/2 in dia, 2-1/2/lb, w/cores and stems	1	166	100	25	1	tr	0.3	1	0	tr
Bosc, 2-1/2 in dia, 3/lb with cores and stems	1	141	85	21	1	tr	0.2	1	0	tr
D'Anjou, 3 in dia, 2/lb w/cores and stems	1	200	120	30	1	tr	0.4	1	0	tr
Pears, canned, fruit and liquid:										
Heavy Syrup Pack	1 cup	255	190	49	1	tr	0.2	tr	0	13

FOOD AND NUTRITION TABLE

Fruits and Juices	amount	grams	calories	carbos g	protein g	sat. fat g	unsat. fat g	fat g	chol mg	sodium mg
Pears, canned, fruit and liquid (cont'd)										
Juice Pack	1 cup	248	125	32	1	tr	tr	tr	0	10
Pineapple, raw, diced	1 cup	155	75	19	1	tr	0.3	1	0	2
Pineapple, canned, fruit and liquid:										
Heavy Syrup Pack, crushed	1 cup	255	200	52	1	tr	0.1	tr	0	3
Slices unsweetened, canned	1 slice	58	45	12	tr	tr	tr	tr	0	3
Plums, raw, w/o pits:										
2-1/2 in dia, 6-1/2/lb in dia, 6-1/2/lb w/pits	1	66	35	9	1	tr	0.4	tr	0	tr
1-1/2 in dia, 15/lb w/pits	1	28	15	4	tr	tr	0.1	tr	0	tr
Prunes, dried:										
Uncooked	4 extra lg	49	115	31	1	tr	0.3	tr	0	2
Cooked, unsweetened, fruit and liquid	1 cup	212	225	60	2	tr	0.4	tr	0	4

FOOD AND NUTRITION TABLE

Fruits and Juices	amount	grams	calories	carbos g	protein g	sat. fat g	unsat. fat g	fat g	chol mg	sodium mg
Raisins, seedless:										
Cup, not pressed down	1 cup	145	435	115	5	0.2	0.2	1	0	17
Packet, 1/2 oz	1 pkt	14	40	11	tr	tr	tr	tr	0	2
Raspberries:										
Raw	1 cup	123	60	14	1	tr	0.5	1	0	tr
Frozen, sweetened	1 cup	250	255	65	2	tr	0.2	tr	0	3
Strawberries:										
Raw, capped, whole	1 cup	149	45	1	10	tr	0.4	1	0	1
Frozen, sweetened, sliced	1 cup	255	245	1	66	tr	0.2	tr	0	8
Tangerines:										
Raw, w/o peel and seeds, 2-3/8 in dia, 4/lb	1	84	35	9	1	tr	tr	tr	0	1
Canned, light syrup	1 cup	252	155	41	1	tr	0.1	tr	0	15

156

FOOD AND NUTRITION TABLE

Fruits and Juices	amount	grams	calories	carbos g	protein g	sat. fat g	unsat. fat g	fat g	chol mg	sodium mg
Watermelon, raw, w/o rind and seeds:										
Piece, 4 by 8 in wedge w/rind and seeds, 1/16th of 32-2/3 lb melon	1 pc	482	155	35	3	0.3	1.2	2	0	10
Watermelon, diced	1 cup	160	50	11	1	0.1	0.4	1	0	3

FOOD AND NUTRITION TABLE

Grain Products	amount	grams	calories	carbos g	protein g	sat. fat g	unsat. fat g	fat g	chol mg	sodium mg
Rice:										
Brown, cooked, served hot	1 cup	195	230	50	5	0.3	0.7	1	0	0
White, enr:										
Comml Varieties:										
Raw	1 cup	185	670	149	12	0.2	0.5	1	0	9
Cooked, served hot	1 cup	205	225	50	4	0.1	0.2	tr	0	0
Instant, ready to serve	1 cup	165	180	40	4	0.1	0.2	0	0	0
Fettuccine, Linguine, Spaghetti, and Vermicelli	2 oz	56	210	42	7	0	0.5	1	0	0

FOOD AND NUTRITION TABLE

Fast Foods	amount	grams	calories	carbos g	protein g	sat. fat g	unsat. fat g	fat g	chol mg	sodium mg
Cheeseburger:										
Regular	1 sand	112	300	28	15	7.3	6.6	15	44	672
4 oz Patty	1 sand	194	525	40	30	15.1	13.6	31	104	1224
Enchilada	1	230	235	24	20	7.7	7.3	16	19	1332
English Muffin, w/egg, cheese, and bacon	1 sand	138	360	31	18	8.0	8.7	18	213	832
Fish Sandwich:										
Regular, w/cheese	1 sand	140	420	39	16	6.3	14.6	23	56	667
Large, w/o cheese	1 sand	170	470	41	18	6.3	18.2	27	91	621
Hamburger:										
Regular	1 sand	98	245	28	12	4.4	5.8	11	32	463
4 oz Patty	1 sand	174	445	38	25	7.1	12.3	21	71	763
Pizza, cheese, 1/8 of 15 in dia pizza	1 slice	120	290	39	15	4.1	3.9	9	56	699
Roast Beef Sandwich	1 sand	150	345	34	22	3.5	8.7	13	55	757
Taco	1	81	195	15	9	4.1	6.3	11	21	456

FOOD AND NUTRITION TABLE

Meats and Meat Products	amount	grams	calories	carbos g	protein g	sat. fat g	unsat. fat g	fat g	chol mg	sodium mg
Beef, cooked, braised, simmered or roasted:										
Chuck, blade:										
Lean and fat, 2-1/2 by 2-1/2 by 3/4 in	3 oz	85	325	0	22	10.8	12.6	26	87	53
Lean Only, from above	2.2 oz	62	170	0	19	3.9	4.5	9	66	44
Bottom Round:										
Lean and fat, 4-1/8 by 2-1/4 by 1/2 in	3 oz	85	220	0	25	4.8	6.2	13	81	43
Lean Only, from above	2.8 oz	78	175	0	25	2.7	3.7	8	75	40
Ground Beef, broiled, patty, 3-in dia by 5/8 in :										
Lean	3 oz	85	230	0	21	6.2	7.5	16	74	65
Regular	3 oz	85	245	0	20	6.9	8.4	18	76	70
Heart, lean, braised	3 oz	85	150	0	24	1.2	2.4	5	164	54
Liver, fried, 6-1/2 by 2-3/8 by 3/8 in	3 oz	85	185	7	23	2.5	4.9	7	410	90

FOOD AND NUTRITION TABLE

Meats and Meat Products	amount	grams	calories	carbos g	protein g	sat. fat g	unsat. fat g	fat g	chol mg	sodium mg
Roast, oven cooked, no liquid added:										
Relatively fat, such as rib:										
Lean and fat, 2 pcs 4-1/8 by 2-1/4 by 1/4 in	3 oz	85	315	0	19	10.8	12.3	26	72	54
Lean Only, from above	2.2 oz	51	150	0	17	3.6	4.0	9	49	45
Relatively Lean, such as eye of the round:										
Lean and fat, 2 pcs 2-1/2 by 2-1/2 by 3/8 in	3 oz	85	205	0	23	4.9	5.9	12	62	50
Lean Only, from above	2.6 oz	75	135	0	22	1.9	2.3	5	52	46
Steak, sirloin, broiled:										
Lean and fat, 1 pc, 2-1/2 by 2-1/2 by 3/4 in	3 oz	85	240	0	23	6.4	7.5	15	77	53
Lean Only, from above	2.5 oz	72	150	0	22	2.6	3.1	6	64	48
Beef, canned, corned	3 oz	85	185	0	22	4.2	5.3	10	80	802
Beef, diced, chipped	2.5 oz	72	145	0	24	1.8	2.2	4	46	3053

FOOD AND NUTRITION TABLE

Meat and Meat Products	amount	grams	calories	carbos g	protein g	sat. fat g	unsat. fat g	fat g	chol mg	sodium mg
Lamb, cooked:										
Chops, (3/lb w/bone):										
Arm, braised:										
Lean and fat	2.2 oz	63	220	0	20	6.9	6.9	15	77	46
Lean Only, from above	1.7 oz	48	135	0	17	2.9	3.0	7	59	36
Loin, broiled:										
Lean and fat	2.8 oz	80	235	0	22	7.3	7.4	16	78	62
Lean Only, from above	2.3 oz	64	140	0	19	2.6	2.8	6	60	54
Leg, roasted:										
Lean and fat, 2 pcs, 4-1/8 by 2-1/4 by 1/4 in	3 oz	85	205	0	22	5.6	5.7	13	78	57
Lean Only, from above	2.6 oz	73	140	0	20	2.4	2.6	6	65	50
Rib, roasted:										
Lean and fat, 3 pcs, 4-1/8 by 2-1/4 by 1/4 in	3 oz	85	315	0	18	12.1	12.1	26	77	60
Lean Only, from above	2 oz	57	130	0	15	3.2	3.5	7	50	46
Pork, cured, cooked:										
Bacon:										
Regular, med. slices	3	19	110	tr	6	3.3	5.6	9	16	303

FOOD AND NUTRITION TABLE

Meat and Meat Products	amount	grams	calories	carbos g	protein g	sat. fat g	unsat. fat g	fat g	chol mg	sodium mg
Bacon (Cont'd):										
Canadian Style, slices	2	46	85	1	11	1.3	2.3	4	27	711
Ham, light cure, roasted:										
Lean and fat, 2 pcs, 4-1/8 by 2-1/4 by 1/4 in	3 oz	85	205	0	18	5.1	8.2	14	53	1009
Lean Only, from above	2.4 oz	68	105	0	17	1.3	2.1	4	37	902
Ham, canned, roasted, 2 pcs, 4-1/2 by 2-1/4 by 1/4 in	3 oz	85	140	tr	18	2.4	4.3	7	35	908
Luncheon Meat:										
Chopped Ham (8 slices per 6 oz pkg)	2 slices	42	95	0	7	2.4	4.3	7	21	576
Cooked Ham (8 slices per 8 oz pkg)										
Regular	2 slices	57	105	2	10	1.9	3.5	6	32	751
Extra Lean	2 slices	57	75	1	11	0.9	1.6	3	27	815

FOOD AND NUTRITION TABLE

Meat and Meat Products	amount	grams	calories	carbos g	protein g	sat. fat g	unsat. fat g	fat g	chol mg	sodium mg
Pork, fresh, cooked:										
Chop, loin, (cut 3/lb w/bone):										
Broiled:										
Lean and fat	3.1 oz	87	275	0	24	7.0	11	19	84	61
Lean Only, from above	2.5 oz	72	165	0	23	2.6	4.3	8	71	56
Pan Fried:										
Lean and fat	3.1 oz	89	335	0	21	9.8	15.6	27	92	64
Lean Only, from above	2.4 oz	67	180	0	19	3.7	6.1	11	72	57
Rib, roasted:										
Lean and fat, 2-1/2 by 3/4 in	3 oz	85	270	0	21	7.2	11.5	20	69	37
Lean Only, from above	2.5 oz	71	175	0	20	3.4	5.6	10	56	33
Shoulder Cut, braised:										
Lean and fat, 3 pcs, 2-1/2 by 2-1/2 by 1/4 in	3 oz	85	295	0	23	7.9	12.4	22	93	75
Lean Only, from above	2.4 oz	67	165	0	22	2.8	4.7	8	76	68
Sausages:										
Bologna, slice, 8/8oz pkg	2 slices	57	180	2	7	6.1	9.0	16	31	581

164

FOOD AND NUTRITION TABLE

Meat and Meat Products	amount	grams	calories	carbos g	protein g	sat. fat g	unsat. fat g	fat g	chol mg	sodium mg
Braunschweiger, slice, 6/6oz pkg	2 slices	57	205	2	8	6.2	10.6	18	89	652
Frankfurter, 10/1lb pkg, cooked (reheated)	1	45	145	1	5	4.8	7.4	13	23	504
Pork Link, 16/1lb pkg,	1	13	50	tr	3	1.4	2.3	4	11	168
Salami:										
Cooked Type, slice, 8/8 oz pkg	2 slices	57	145	1	8	4.6	6.4	11	37	607
Dry Type, slice, 12/4oz pkg	2 slices	20	85	1	5	2.4	4.0	7	16	372
Vienna Sausage, 7/4 oz can	1 sausage	16	45	tr	2	1.5	2.3	4	8	152
Veal, med fat, cooked, bone removed:										
Cutlet, 4-1/8 by 2-1/4 by 1/2 in, braised or broiled	3 oz	85	185	0	23	4.1	4.7	9	109	56
Rib, 2 pcs, 4-1/8 by 2-1/4 by 1/4 in, roasted	3 oz	85	230	0	23	6.0	7.0	14	109	57

FOOD AND NUTRITION TABLE

Meat and Meat Products	amount	grams	calories	carbos g	protein g	sat. fat g	unsat. fat g	fat g	chol mg	sodium mg
Mixed Dishes										
Beef and Vegetable Stew (home recipe)	1 cup	245	220	15	16	4.4	5.0	11	71	292
Beef Potpie, baked, 1/3 of 9 in dia pie (home recipe)	1 pc	210	515	39	21	7.9	20.3	30	42	596
Chicken and Noodles, cooked (home recipe)	1 cup	240	365	26	22	5.1	11	18	103	600
Chicken Chow Mein:										
Canned	1 cup	250	95	18	7	0.1	0.9	tr	8	725
Home Recipe	1 cup	250	255	10	31	4.1	8.4	10	75	718
Chicken Potpie, baked, 1/3 of 9 in dia pie, home recipe	1 pc	232	545	42	23	10.3	22.1	31	56	594
Chili Con Carne, w/beans, canned	1 cup	255	340	31	19	5.8	8.2	16	28	1354
Macaroni, enr, and Cheese, (home recipe), w/marg	1 cup	200	430	40	17	9.8	11.1	22	44	1086

FOOD AND NUTRITION TABLE

Meat and Meat Products	amount	grams	calories	carbos g	protein g	sat. fat g	unsat. fat g	fat g	chol mg	sodium mg
Mixed Dishes										
Spaghetti, enr, w/tomato sauce and cheese:										
Canned	1 cup	250	190	39	6	0.4	0.9	2	3	955
Home Recipe	1 cup	250	260	37	9	3.0	4.8	9	8	955
Spaghetti, enr, w/meat balls and tomato sauce:										
Canned	1 cup	250	260	29	12	2.4	7.0	10	23	1220
Home Recipe	1 cup	248	330	39	19	3.9	6.6	12	89	1009

FOOD AND NUTRITION TABLE

Nuts, Seeds, and Legumes	amount	grams	calories	carbos g	protein g	sat. fat g	unsat. fat g	fat g	chol mg	sodium mg
Almonds, shelled:										
Slivered, packed	1 cup	135	795	28	27	6.7	60.6	70.	0	15
Whole	1 oz	28	165	6	6	1.4	12.7	15.	0	3
Beans, dry:										
Cooked, drained:										
Black	1 cup	171	225	41	15	0.1	0.6	1.	0	1
Great Northern	1 cup	180	210	38	14	0.1	0.7	1.	0	13
Lima	1 cup	19	260	49	16	0.2	0.6	1.	0	4
Pea (navy)	1 cup	190	225	40	15	0.1	0.8	1.	0	13
Pinto	1 cup	180	265	49	15	0.1	0.6	1.	0	3
Black-Eyed Peas, dry, cooked (w/residual cooking liquid)	1 cup	250	190	35	13	0.2	0.3	1.	0	20
Brazil Nuts, shelled	1 oz	28	185	4	4	4.6	13.3	19.	0	1
Cashew Nuts, salted:										
Dry Roasted	1 cup	137	785	45	21	12.5	48.1	63.	0	877*
	1 oz	28	165	9	4	2.6	9.9	13.	0	181*
Roasted in Oil	1 cup	130	750	37	21	12.4	47.5	63.	0	814**

*Cashews w/o salt contain 21 mg sodium/cup or 4 mg/oz.
** Cashews w/salt contain 22 mg soduim/cup or 5 mg/oz

FOOD AND NUTRITION TABLE

Nuts, Seeds, and Legumes	amount	grams	calories	carbos g	protein g	sat. fat g	unsat. fat g	fat g	chol mg	sodium mg
Cashew Nuts, salted (Cont'd):										
Roasted in Oil	1 oz	28	165	8	5	2.7	10.4	14	0	177**
Chickpeas, cooked, drained	1 cup	163	270	45	15	0.4	2.8	4	0	11
Coconut:										
Raw, shredded or grated	1 cup	80	285	12	3	23.8	1.4	27	0	16
Dried, sweetened, shredded	1 cup	93	470	44	3	29.3	1.8	33	0	244
Filberts, (hazelnuts),	1 cup	115	725	18	15	5.3	63.4	72	0	3
	1 oz	28	180	4	4	1.3	15.6	18	0	1
Lentils, dry, cooked	1 cup	200	215	38	16	0.1	0.7	1	0	26
Mixed Nuts, w/peanuts, salted:										
Dry Roasted	1 oz	28	170	7	5	2.0	12	15	0	180*
Roasted in Oil	1 oz	28	175	6	5	2.5	12.8	16	0	185*
Peanuts, roasted in oil,	1 cup	145	840	27	39	9.9	58.1	71	0	626**
	1 oz	28	165	5	8	1.9	11.3	14	0	122**

* Mixed nuts w/o salt contain 3 mg sodium/oz.
** Peanuts w/o salt contain 22 mg sodium/cup or 4 mg/oz.

FOOD AND NUTRITION TABLE

Nuts, Seeds, and Legumes	amount	grams	calories	carbos g	protein g	sat. fat g	unsat. fat g	fat g	chol mg	sodium mg
Peanut Butter	1 tbsp	16	95	3	5	1.4	6.5	8	0	75
Peas, Split, dry, cooked	1 cup	200	230	42	16	0.1	0.4	1	0	26
Pecans, halves	1 cup	108	720	20	8	5.9	63.6	73	0	1
Pistachio Nuts, dried, shelled	1 oz	28	190	5	2	1.5	16.7	19	0	tr
	1 oz	28	165	7	6	1.7	11.4	14	0	2
Refried Beans, canned	1 cup	290	295	51	18	0.4	2.0	3	0	1228
Sesame Seeds, dry, hulled	1 tbsp	8	45	1	2	0.6	3.6	4	0	3
Tofu, piece 2-1/2 by 2-3/4 by 1 in	1 pc	120	85	3	9	0.7	3.9	5	0	8
Walnuts, black, chopped	1 cup	125	760	15	30	4.5	62.8	71	0	1
	1 oz	28	170	3	7	1.0	14.2	16	0	tr
Walnuts, English, pcs or chips	1 cup	128	770	22	17	6.7	64	74	0	12
	1 oz	28	180	5	4	1.6	15.1	18	0	3

FOOD AND NUTRITION TABLE

Oils and Shortenings	amount	grams	calories	carbos g	protein g	sat. fat g	unsat. fat g	fat g	chol mg	sodium mg
Butter (4 sticks/lb):										
Stick	1/2 cup	113	810	tr	1	57.1	29.8	92	247	933*
Tablespoon (1/8 stick)	1 tbsp	14	100	tr	tr	7.1	3.7	11	31	116*
Pat, 1/2 in sq by 1/3 in	1 pat	5	35	tr	tr	2.5	1.4	4	11	41*
Fats, vegetable shortenings	1 cup	205	1810	0	0	51.3	144.7	205	0	0
	1 tbsp	13	115	0	0	3.3	9.2	13	0	0
Lard	1 cup	205	1850	0	0	80.4	115.5	205	195	0
	1 tbsp	13	115	0	0	5.1	7.4	13	12	0
Margarine:										
Regular (about 80% fat):										
Hard (4 sticks/lb):										
Stick	1/2 cup	113	810	1	1	17.9	69.2	91	0	1066**
Tablespoon (1/8 stick)	1 tbap	14	100	tr	tr	2.2	8.6	11	0	132**
Pat, 1 in sq by 1/3 in	1 pat	5	35	tr	tr	0.8	3.1	4	0	47**
Soft	8 oz contr	227	1625	1	2	31.3	143.2	183	0	2449**
	1 tbsp	14	100	tr	tr	1.9	8.8	11	0	151**

* For salted butter, unsalted butter contains 12 mg sodium/stick, 2 mg/tbsp, or 1 mg/pat
** For salted margarine

FOOD AND NUTRITION TABLE

Oils and Shortenings	amount	grams	calories	carbos g	protein g	sat. fat g	unsat. fat g	fat g	chol mg	sodium mg
Oils, salad or cooking:										
Corn	1 cup	218	1925	0	0	27.7	180.8	218	0	0
	1 tbsp	14	125	0	0	1.8	11.6	14	0	0
Olive	1 cup									
	1 tbsp	14	125	0	0	1.9	11.5	14	0	0
Peanut	1 cup	216	1910	0	0	36.5	168.9	216	0	0
	1 tbsp	14	125	0	0	2.4	11.0	14	0	0
Safflower	1 cup	218	1925	0	0	19.8	188.8	218	0	0
	1 tbsp	14	125	0	0	1.3	12.1	14	0	0
Salad Dressings:										
Commercial:										
Blue Cheese	1 tbsp	15	75	1	1	1.5	6.0	8	3	164
French:										
Regular	1 tbsp	16	85	1	tr	1.4	7.5	9	0	188
Low Calorie	1 tbsp	16	25	2	tr	0.2	1.3	2	0	306
Italian:										
Regular	1 tbsp	15	80	1	tr	1.3	6.9	9	0	162
Low Calorie	1 tbsp	15	5	2	tr	tr	tr	tr	0	136

FOOD AND NUTRITION TABLE

Oils and Shortenings	amount	grams	calories	carbos g	protein g	sat. fat g	unsat. fat g	fat g	chol mg	sodium mg
Salad Dressings (Cont'd)										
Mayonnaise:										
Regular	1 tbsp	14	100	tr	tr	1.7	9.0	11	8	80
Imitation	1 tbsp	15	35	2	tr	0.5	2.3	3	4	75
Tarter Sauce	1 tbsp	14	75	1	tr	1.2	6.5	8	4	182
Thousand Island:										
Regular	1 tbsp	16	60	2	tr	1.0	4.5	6	4	112
Low Calorie	1 tbsp	15	25	2	tr	0.2	1.3	2	2	150
Vinegar and Oil, (home recipe)	1 tbsp	16	70	tr	0	1.5	6.3	8	0	tr

FOOD AND NUTRITION TABLE

Poultry, Poultry Products	amount	grams	calories	carbos g	protein g	sat. fat g	unsat. fat g	fat g	chol mg	sodium mg
Chicken:										
Fried, flesh w/skin:										
Batter Dipped:										
Breast, 1/2 breast, 5.6 oz, w/bones	4.9 oz	140	365	13	35	.9	11.9	18.	119	395
Drumstick, 3/4 oz, w/bones	2.5 oz	72	195	6	16	3.0	7.3	11	62	194
Floured:										
Breast, 1/2 breast, 4.2 oz, w/bones	3.5 oz	98	220	2	31	2.4	5.3	9.	87	74
Drumstick, 2.6 oz, w/bones	1.7 oz	49	120	1	13	1.8	4.3	7.	44	44
Roasted, flesh only:										
Breast, 1/2 breast, 4.2 oz, w/bones and skin	3.0 oz	86	140	0	27	0.9	1.8	3.	73	64
Drumstick, 2.9 oz, w/bones and skin	1.6 oz	44	75	0	12	0.7	1.4	2.	41	42
Stewed, flesh only, light and dark meat, chopped or diced	1 cup	140	250	0	38	2.6	5.5	9.	116	98
Chicken Liver, cooked	1 liver	20	30	tr	5	0.4	0.5	1.	126	10

FOOD AND NUTRITION TABLE

Poultry, Poultry Products	amount	grams	calories	carbos g	protein g	sat. fat g	unsat. fat g	fat g	chol mg	sodium mg
Duck, roasted, flesh only	1/2 duck	221	445	0	52	9.2	11.4	25	197	144
Turkey, roasted, flesh only:										
Dark Meat, 2-1/2 by 1-5/8 by1/4 in piece	4 pcs	85	160	0	24	2.1	3.2	6	72	67
Turkey, roasted, flesh only (Cont'd):										
Light Meat, 4 by 2 by 1/4 in piece	2 pcs	85	135	0	25	0.9	1.2	3	59	54
Light and Dark Meat: Chopped or Diced	1 cup	140	240	0	41	2.3	3.4	7	106	98
Poultry Food Products:										
Chicken:										
Frankfurter, 10/lb pkg	1 frank	45	115	3	6	2.5	5.6	9	45	616
Roll, light, 6 slices/ 6 oz pkg	2 slices	57	90	1	11	1.1	2.6	4	28	331
Turkey:										
Gravy and Turkey, frozen	5 oz pkg	142	95	7	8	1.2	2.1	4	26	787
Loaf, breast meat, 8 slices/ 6 oz pkg	2 slices	42	45	0	10	0.2	0.3	1	17	608

FOOD AND NUTRITION TABLE

Poultry, Poultry Products	amount	grams	calories	carbos g	protein g	sat. fat g	unsat. fat g	fat g	chol mg	sodium mg
Turkey: Roast, boneless, frozen, seasoned, light and dark meat, cooked	3 oz	85	130	3	18	1.6	2.4	5	45	578

FOOD AND NUTRITION TABLE

Soups, Sauces, and Gravies	amount	grams	calories	carbos g	protein g	sat. fat g	unsat. fat g	fat g	chol mg	sodium mg
Soup, canned, condensed:*										
Clam Chowder, New England	1 cup	248	165	17	9	3.0	3.4	7	22	992
Cream of Chicken	1 cup	248	190	15	7	4.6	6.1	11	27	1047
Cream of Mushroom	1 cup	248	205	15	6	5.1	7.6	14	20	1076
Tomato	1 cup	248	160	22	6	2.9	2.7	6	17	932
Soups, canned, condensed:**										
Beans and Bacon	1 cup	253	170	23	8	1.5	4.0	6	3	951
Beef Broth, bouillon, consomme	1 cup	240	15	tr	3	0.3	0.2	1	tr	782
Beef Noodle	1 cup	244	85	9	5	1.1	1.7	3	5	952
Chicken Noodle	1 cup	241	75	9	4	0.7	1.7	2	7	1106
Chicken Rice	1 cup	241	60	7	4	0.5	1.3	2	7	815
Cream of Chicken	1 cup	244	115	9	3	2.1	4.8	7	10	986
Cream of Mushroom	1 cup	244	130	9	2	2.4	5.9	9	2	1032
Minestrone	1 cup	241	80	11	4	0.6	1.8	3	2	911
Pea, green	1 cup	250	165	27	9	1.4	1.4	3	0	988

*Prepared with an equal volume of milk.
**Prepare with an equal volume of water.

FOOD AND NUTRITION TABLE

Soups, Sauces, and Gravies	amount	grams	calories	carbos g	protein g	sat. fat g	unsat. fat g	fat g	chol mg	sodium mg
Tomato	1 cup	244	85	17	2	0.4	1.4	2	0	871
Vegetable Beef	1 cup	244	80	10	2	0.9	0.9	2	5	956
Vegetarian	1 cup	241	70	2	12	0.3	1.5	2	0	822
Soups, dehydrated, prepared w/water:										
Chicken Noodle, 1 pkt	6 fl oz	188	40	6	2	0.2	0.7	1	2	957
Onion, 1 pkt	6 fl oz	184	20	4	1	0.1	0.3	tr	0	635
Tomato Vegetable, 1 pkt	6 fl oz	189	40	8	1	0.3	0.3	1	0	856
Sauces:										
From dry mix:										
Cheese prepare w/milk	1 cup	279	305	23	16	9.3	6.9	17	53	1565
Hollandaise, prepared w/water	1 cup	259	240	14	5	11.6	6.8	20	52	1564
White Sauce, prepared w/milk	1 cup	264	240	21	10	6.4	6.4	13	34	797

FOOD AND NUTRITION TABLE

Soups, Sauces, and Gravies	amount	grams	calories	carbos g	protein g	sat. fat g	unsat. fat g	fat g	chol mg	sodium mg
Sauces:										
From Dry Mix:										
From Home Recipe:										
White Sauce, med*	1 cup	250	395	24	10	9.1	19.1	30	32	888
Read to Serve:										
Barbecue	1 tbsp	16	10	2	tr	tr	0.2	tr	0	130
Soy	1 tbsp	18	10	2	2	0	0	0	0	1029
Gravies										
Gravies, canned:										
Beef	1 cup	233	125	11	9	2.7	2.5	5	7	1305
Chicken	1 cup	238	190	13	5	3.4	9.7	14	5	1373
Mushroom	1 cup	238	120	13	3	1.0	5.2	6	0	1357
Gravies, from dry mix:										
Brown	1 cup	261	80	14	3	0.9	0.9	2	2	1147
Chicken	1 cup	360	85	14	3	0.5	1.3	2	3	1134

*Prepared with an equal volume of milk.

FOOD AND NUTRITION TABLE

Sugars and Sweets	amount	grams	calories	carbos g	protein g	sat. fat g	unsat. fat g	fat g	chol mg	sodium mg
Candy:										
Caramels, plain or chocolate	1 oz	28	115	22	1	2.2	0.4	3	1	64
Chocolate:										
Milk, plain	1 oz	28	145	16	2	5.4	3.3	9	6	23
Milk, w/almonds	1 oz	28	150	15	3	4.8	4.8	10	5	23
Milk, w/peanuts	1 oz	28	155	13	4	4.2	5.0	11	5	19
Milk, w/rice cereal	1 oz	28	140	18	2	4.4	2.7	7	6	46
Semisweet, pcs, (60/oz)	1 cup	170	860	97	7	36.2	21.8	61	0	24
Sweet, dark	1 oz	28	150	16	1	5.9	3.6	10	0	5
Fudge, chocolate, plain	1 oz	28	115	21	1	2.1	1.1	3	1	54
Gum Drops	1 oz	28	100	25	tr	tr	0.1	tr	0	10
Hard Candy	1 oz	28	110	28	0	0	0	0	0	7
Jelly Beans	1 oz	28	105	26	tr	tr	0.1	tr	0	7
Marshmallows	1 oz	28	90	33	1	0	0	0	0	25
Custard, baked	1 cup	265	305	29	14	6.8	6.1	15	278	209
Gelatin Dessert, prepared w/gelatin dessert powder and water	1/2 cup	120	70	17	2	0	0	0	0	55

FOOD AND NUTRITION TABLE

Sugars and Sweets	amount	grams	calories	carbos g	protein g	sat. fat g	unsat. fat g	fat g	chol mg	sodium mg
Honey, strained or extracted	1 cup	339	1030	279	1	0	0	0	0	17
	1 tbsp	21	65	17	tr	0	0	0	0	1
Jams and Preserves	1 tbsp	20	55	14	tr	0	tr	tr	0	2
	1 pkt	14	40	10	tr	0	tr	tr	0	2
Jellies	1 tbsp	18	50	13	tr	tr	tr	tr	0	5
	1 pkt	14	40	10	tr	tr	tr	tr	0	4
Popsicle, 3/12 fl oz size	1	95	70	18	0	0	0	0	0	11
Puddings: Canned:										
Chocolate	5 oz can	142	205	30	3	9.5	0.6	11	1	285
Tapioca	5 oz can	142	160	28	3	4.8	tr	5	tr	252
Vanilla	5 oz can	142	220	33	2	9.5	0.3	10	1	305
Dry Mix, prepared w/whole milk;										
Chocolate Instant	1/2 cup	130	155	27	4	2.3	1.3	4	14	440
Regular, cooked	1/2 cup	130	150	25	4	2.4	1.2	4	15	167
Rice	1/2 cup	132	155	27	4	2.3	1.2	4	15	140
Tapioca	1/2 cup	130	145	25	4	2.3	1.2	4	15	152

FOOD AND NUTRITION TABLE

Sugars and Sweets	amount	grams	calories	carbos g	protein g	sat. fat g	unsat. fat g	fat g	chol mg	sodium mg
Vanilla:										
Instant	1/2 cup	130	150	27	4	2.2	1.8	4	15	375
Regular, cooked	1/2 cup	130	145	25	4	2.3	1.1	4	15	178
Sugars:										
Brown, pressed down	1 cup	220	820	212	0	0	0	0	0	97
White:										
Granulated	1 cup	200	770	199	0	0	0	0	0	5
	1 tbsp	12	45	12	0	0	0	0	0	t
Powdered, sifted, spooned into cup	1 cup	100	385	6	0	0	0	0	0	tr
Syrups:										
Chocolate Flavored Syrup or Topping:										
Thin Type	2 tbsp	38	85	22	1	0.2	0.2	tr	0	36
Fudge Type	2 tbsp	38	125	21	2	3.1	1.9	5	0	42
Molasses, cane, blackstrap	2 tbsp	40	85	22	0	0	0	0	0	38
Table Syrup, corn and maple	2 tbsp	42	122	32	0	0	0	0	0	19

FOOD AND NUTRITION TABLE

Vegetables	amount	grams	calories	carbos g	protein g	sat. fat g	unsat. fat g	fat g	chol mg	sodium mg
Artichokes, cooked, drained	1	120	55	12	3	tr	0.1	tr	0	79
Asparagus, green:										
Cooked, drained:										
From Raw:										
Cuts and Tips	1 cup	180	45	8	5	0.1	0.2	1	0	7
Spears, 1/2 in dia at base	4 spears	60	15	3	2	tr	0.1	tr	0	2
From Frozen:										
Cuts and Tips	1 cup	180	50	9	5	0.2	0.3	1	0	7
Spears, 1/2 in dia at base	4 spears	60	15	3	2	0.1	0.1	1	0	2
Bamboo Shoots, canned, drained	1 cup	131	25	4	2	0.1	0.2	1	0	9
Beans:										
Lima, frozen, cooked, drained:										
Thick-Seeded Type	1 cup	170	170	32	10	0.1	0.3	1	0	90
Thin-Seeded Type, baby limas	1 cup	180	190	35	12	0.1	0.3	1	0	52

FOOD AND NUTRITION TABLE

Vegetables	amount	grams	calories	carbos g	protein g	sat. fat g	unsat. fat g	fat g	chol mg	sodium mg
Beans (Cont'd):										
Snap, cooked, drained:										
From Raw, cut and French style	1 cup	125	45	10	2	0.1	0.2	tr	0	4
From Frozen, cut	1 cup	135	35	8	2	tr	0.1	tr	0	18
Bean Sprouts, mung:										
Raw	1 cup	104	30	6	3	tr	0.1	tr	0	6
Cooked, drained	1 cup	124	25	5	3	tr	tr	tr	0	12
Beets:										
Cooked, drained:										
Diced or Sliced	1 cup	170	55	11	2	tr	tr	tr	0	83
Whole, 2 in dia	2 beets	100	30	7	1	tr	tr	tr	0	49
Canned, drained solids, diced or sliced	1 cup	170	55	12	2	tr	0.1	tr	0	466*

*For regular pack; special dietary pack contains 78 mg sodium.

FOOD AND NUTRITION TABLE

Vegetables	amount	grams	calories	carbos g	protein g	sat. fat g	unsat. fat g	fat g	chol mg	sodium mg
Black-Eyed Peas, immature, seeds, cooked and drained:										
From Raw										
From Frozen										
Broccoli:										
Cooked and drained:										
From Raw:										
Spear Medium	1 spear	180	50	10	5	0.1	0.2	1	0	20
Spears, cut into 1/2 in pcs	1 cup	155	45	9	5	0.1	0.2	tr	0	17
From Frozen:										
Piece, 4-1/2 to 5 in long	1 pc	30	10	2	1	tr	tr	tr	0	7
Chopped	1 cup	185	50	10	6	tr	0.1	tr	0	44
Brussels Sprouts, cooked and drained:										
From Raw, 7 to 8 sprouts 1-1/4 to 1-1/2 in dia	1 cup	155	60	13	4	0.2	0.5	1	0	33

FOOD AND NUTRITION TABLE

Vegetables	amount	grams	calories	carbos g	protein g	sat. fat g	unsat. fat g	fat g	chol mg	sodium mg
Brussels Sprouts, cooked and drained (cont'd):										
From Frozen	1 cup	155	65	13	6	0.1	0.3	1	0	36
Caabbage, common varieties:										
Raw, coursely shredded or sliced	1 cup	70	15	4	1	tr	0.1	tr	0	13
Cooked, drained	1 cup	150	30	7	1	tr	0.2	tr	0	29
Cabbage, Chinese:										
Bak-Choi, cooked, drained	1 cup	170	20	3	3	tr	0.1	tr	0	58
Cabbage, red, raw, coarsely shredded or diced	1 cup	70	20	4	1	tr	0.1	tr	0	8
Carrots:										
Raw, w/o crowns and tips, scraped:										
Whole, 7-1/2 by 1-1/8 dia	1 carrot	72	30	7	1	tr	0.1	tr	0	25
Grated	1 cup	10	45	11	1	tr	0.1	tr	0	39
Cooked, sliced, drained:										
From Raw	1 cup	156	70	16	2	0.1	0.1	tr	0	103
From Frozen	1 cup	146	55	12	2	tr	0.1	tr	0	86

FOOD AND NUTRITION TABLE

Vegetables	amount	grams	calories	carbos g	protein g	sat. fat g	unsat. fat g	fat g	chol mg	sodium mg
Cauliflower:										
Raw, flowerets	1 cup	100	25	5	2	tr	0.1	tr	0	15
Cooked, drained:										
From Raw, flowerets	1 cup	125	30	6	2	tr	0.1	tr	0	8
From Frozen, flowerets	1 cup	180	35	7	3	0.1	0.2	tr	0	32
Celery, pascal type, raw:										
Stalk, large outer, 8 by 1-1/2 at root end	1 stalk	40	5	1	tr	tr	tr	tr	0	35
Pieces, diced	1 cup	120	20	4	1	tr	0.1	tr	0	106
Collards, cooked, drained:										
From Raw, w/o stems	1 cup	190	25	5	2	0.1	0.2	tr	0	36
From Frozen, chopped	1 cup	170	60	12	5	0.1	0.5	1	0	85
Corn, sweet:										
Cooked, drained:										
From Raw, ear 5 by 1-3/4 in	1 ear	77	85	19	3	0.2	0.8	1	0	13
From Frozen:										
Ear, trimmed to 3-1/2 in lg	1 ear	63	60	14	2	0.1	0.3	tr	0	3
Kernels	1 cup	165	135	34	5	tr	0.1	tr	0	8

FOOD AND NUTRITION TABLE

Vegetables	amount	grams	calories	carbos g	protein g	sat. fat g	unsat. fat g	fat g	chol mg	sodium mg
Corn, sweet:										
Canned (Cont'd):										
Cream Style	1 cup	256	185	46	4	0.2	0.8	1	0	730*
Whole Kernel, vacuum pack	1 cup	210	165	41	5	0.2	0.8	1	0	571**
Cucumber, w/peel, 1/8 in thick, slices 2-1/8 in dia	6 slices	28	5	1	tr	tr	tr	tr	0	1
Eggplant, cooked, steamed	1 cup	96	25	6	1	tr	0.1	tr	0	3
Endive, curly, small raw pieces	1 cup	50	10	2	1	tr	tr	tr	0	11
Lettuce, raw:										
Bottom Types:										
Head, 5 in dia	1 head	163	20	4	2	tr	0.2	tr	0	8
Leaves	1 outer 2 inner	15	tr	tr	tr	tr	tr	tr	0	1
Iceberg:										
Head, 6 in dia	1 head	539	70	11	5	0.1	0.5	1	0	49
Wedge, 1/4 of head	1 wedge	135	20	3	1	tr	0.1	tr	0	12

*For regular pack; special dietary pack contains 8 mg sodium.
**For regular pack; special dietary pack contains 6 mg sodium.

FOOD AND NUTRITION TABLE

Vegetables	amount	grams	calories	carbos g	protein g	sat. fat g	unsat. fat g	fat g	chol mg	sodium mg
Lettuce, raw (Cont'd):										
Romaine, looseleaf, chopped or shredded pcs	1 cup	56	10	2	1	tr	0.1	tr	0	5
Mushrooms:										
Raw, sliced or chopped	1 cup	70	20	3	1	tr	0.1	tr	0	3
Cooked, drained	1 cup	156	40	8	3	0.1	0.3	1	0	3
Canned, drained solids	1 cup	156	35	8	3	0.1	0.2	tr	0	663
Okra Pods, 3 by 5/8 in, cooked	8 pods	85	25	6	2	tr	tr	tr	0	4
Onions:										
Raw:										
Chopped	1 cup	160	55	12	2	0.1	0.3	tr	0	3
Sliced	1 cup	115	40	8	1	0.1	0.1	tr	0	2
Cooked, whole or sliced drained	1 cup	210	60	13	2	0.1	0.1	tr	0	17
Onions, spring raw, white portion, 3/8 in dia	6 onions	30	10	2	1	1.7	tr	tr	0	1

FOOD AND NUTRITION TABLE

Vegetables	amount	grams	calories	carbos g	protein g	sat. fat g	unsat. fat g	fat g	chol mg	sodium mg
Onion Rings, breaded, par-fried, frozen, prepared	2 rings	20	80	8	1	1.7	3.2	5	0	75
Peas, edible pod, cooked, drained	1 cup	160	65	11	5	0.1	0.2	tr	0	6
Peas, green:										
Canned, drained solids	1 cup	170	115	21	8	0.1	0.4	1	0	372*
Frozen, cooked, drained	1 cup	160	125	23	8	0.1	0.2	tr	0	139
Peppers:										
Hot Chili, raw	1 pepper	45	20	4	1	tr	tr	tr	0	3
Sweet, about 5/lb whole, w/o stems and seeds:										
Raw	1 pepper	74	20	4	1	tr	0.2	tr	0	2
Cooked, drained	1 pepper	73	15	3	tr	tr	0.1	tr	0	1
Potatoes, cooked:										
Baked, about 2/lb raw:										
With Skin	1 potato	202	220	51	5	0.1	0.1	tr	0	16
Without Skin	1 potato	156	145	34	3	tr	0.1	tr	0	8

*For regular Pack; special dietary pack contains 3 mg sodium.

FOOD AND NUTRITION TABLE

Vegetables	amount	grams	calories	carbos g	protein g	sat. fat g	unsat. fat g	fat g	chol mg	sodium mg
Potatoes, cooked:										
Boiled, about 3/lb, raw										
Peeled After Boiling	1 potato	136	120	27	3	tr	0.1	tr	0	5
Peeled Before Boiling	1 potato	135	115	27	2	tr	0.1	tr	0	7
French Fried, frozen, 2 to 3-1/2 in long:										
Oven Heated	10 pcs	50	110	17	2	2.1	2.1	4	0	16
Fried in Veg Oil	10 pcs	50	160	20	2	2.5	5.4	8	0	108
Potato Products, prepared:										
Potatoes Au Gratin:										
From Dry Mix	1 cup	245	230	31	6	6.3	3.2	10	12	1076
From Home Recipe	1 cup	245	325	28	12	11.6	6.0	19	56	1061
Hash Browns, from frozen	1 cup	156	340	44	5	7.0	10.1	18	0	51
Mashed:										
From Home Recipe:										
Milk Added	1 cup	210	160	37	4	0.7	0.4	1	4	636
Milk and Margarine Added	1 cup	210	225	35	4	2.2	6.2	9	4	620

FOOD AND NUTRITION TABLE

Vegetables	amount	grams	calories	carbos g	protein g	sat. fat g	unsat. fat g	fat g	chol mg	sodium mg
Potato Products (Cont'd):										
Potato Salad, made w/mayo	1 cup	250	360	28	7	3.6	15.5	21	170	1323
Scalloped:										
From Dry Mix	1 cup	245	230	31	5	6.5	3.5	11	27	835
From Home Recipe	1 cup	245	210	26	7	5.5	2.9	9	29	821
Potato Chips	10 chips	20	105	10	1	1.8	4.8	7	0	94
Potato Chips, cooked w/Olestra	17 chips	28	75	17	2	0	0	0	0	200
Radishes, raw, ends and rootlets cut off	4	18	5	1	tr	tr	tr	tr	0	4
Sauerkraut, canned, solids and liquid	1 cup	236	45	10	2	0.1	0.1	tr	0	1560
Spinach:										
Raw, chopped	1 cup	55	10	2	2	tr	0.1	tr	0	43
Cooked, drained:										
From Raw	1 cup	180	40	7	5	0.1	0.2	tr	0	126
From Frozen, leaf	1 cup	190	55	10	6	0.1	0.2	tr	0	163
Canned, drained solids	1 cup	214	50	7	6	0.2	0.4	1	0	683*

*With added salt; if none is added, sodium content is 58 mg.

FOOD AND NUTRITION TABLE

Vegetables	amount	grams	calories	carbos g	protein g	sat. fat g	unsat. fat g	fat g	chol mg	sodium mg
Spinach Souffle	1 cup	136	220	3	11	7.1	9.9	18	184	763
Sweetpotatoes:										
Cooked, raw, 5 by 2 in, about 2-1/2/lb:										
Baked in Skin, peeled	1 potato	114	115	28	2	tr	0.1	tr	0	11
Baked w/o Skin	1 potato	151	160	37	2	0.1	0.2	tr	0	20
Candied	1 pc	105	145	29	1	1.4	0.9	3	8	74
Tomatoes:										
Raw, 2-3/5 in dia (about 4 oz)	1 tomato	123	25	5	1	tr	0.1	tr	0	10
Canned, solids and liquid	1 cup	240	50	10	2	0.1	0.3	1	0	391*
Tomato Products, canned:										
Paste	1 cup	262	220	49	10	0.3	1.3	2	0	170
Puree	1 cup	250	105	25	4	tr	0.1	tr	0	50
Sauce	1 cup	245	75	18	3	0.1	0.3	tr	0	1482**

*For regular pack; special dietary-pack contains 31 mg sodium.
**With salt added.